Updates on the Journey
It's All About Love, Isn't It?

by
Mukti
Leslye Lawrence

Updates on the Journey:
It's All About Love, Isn't It?

First Printing 2023

ISBN 978-1-329-17237-1

Chamakanda Press

Updates on the Journey

It's All About Love, Isn't It?

by
Mukti
Leslye Lawrence

Introduction
by Stephen Spitalny

Leslye Lawrence met her teacher, Baba Hari Dass, when she was a teenager. As you will read in this collection of writings, that meeting changed the trajectory of her life. Along they way, Baba Hari Dass gave her the name *Mukti*, which means liberation. This naming was apt because it became more and more clear that it was her path to grapple with becoming free from attachment and accepting of impermanence. She danced between doubt and trust on this journey.

from Baba Hari Dass

Every second of our lives is like a seed of grain,
and time is a hungry bird eating
every seed very quickly. When the grain is finished
the bird will fly away. So worship
God, surrender to God, and attain peace.

*

Before attaining liberation, you have to forget all
you have learned. Liberation is
beyond learning.

*

Fear of death is the root of all fears. One who has
removed that fear is liberated.

*

Birth and death are as real as sunrise and sunset.
Birth is celebrated by cheers of
happiness, but death is faced by fear and
mourning. Birth is seen as a moment of
happiness and death appears as a great tragedy.
But both are two ends of the
same rope.

The descent of God into a human form is a God-incarnated soul. Realization of the
God within is the liberation of the human soul.

*

When Leslye and I first got together, one of the things she made sure I understood was that when she was dying (this was 18 years before her cancer diagnosis) she would need help letting go of this life. She wanted me to be prepared to assure her that it would be ok to go, to let go.

Her last 3 and a half years were an accelerated process of coming to terms with impermanence, with inevitable death, with liberation. She was, however, human and she oscillated between acceptance and resistance. In the end, she embraced impermanence and the possibility inherent in being human. In her last coherent moment she took my hand in hers, and put her other hand on my cheek and spoke these words:

"It's all about love, isn't it?"

Her journey can serve as a powerful teaching for all of us if we are open.

In our culture, we have allowed death to be related to as something to be avoided with whatever efforts necessary. We frame life as a battle against illness, attempting to hold off death at all costs. Life is seen as a struggle against death. We become so attached to life and we reject death.

We tend to ignore that death and life are on the same team, they are siblings - birth, life and death. We come in through one door, and go out the other. And we travel from one to the other. There is no other path than towards death's door. It is more inevitable than taxes. Fully embracing this, accepting this, is an aspect of the non-attachment that all spiritual tradition points us toward.

One of the amazing things about Leslye/Mukti, is that in facing her upcoming appointment with death, she invited us along for the journey with transparent honesty. She used her disease as an opportunity to discover more about life, and to welcome life as it is with gratitude. Some say she was courageous. What is courage? It is not without fear, it is not without suffering. From day to day, its is fluid, unpredictable like a rollercoaster ride if you were blindfolded.

What I experienced was the revelation of an amazing being who was sparkling, funny, smart, dedicated, strong, a truly amazing listener, caring and compassionate, passionate about what needs to change in the world, warm, loving and generally wonderful as she approached the inevitable ending of her life in a physical body. For all my time with her, I saw someone who continuously tried to make of herself a better person *as she saw fit.* And the disease accelerated her process.

She made dying, for me, so much less daunting and in fact, something I have become willing to consider, to accept as something that stands ahead of me, stands ahead of each one of us.

Leslye wanted her writings, her ramblings as she called them, collected and accessible so we can all smile and cry together. She supremely doubted her ability to express coherently in writing, but you, the reader, will see otherwise. She was in fact articulate, perceptive and very wise.

She always showed her writing to me, full of self doubt, asking for content editing. Over and over I corrected typos and told her that what she had written was powerful, important and did not need editing. She was expressing very clearly what she was experiencing, and it was important for others to read.

And what has happened now that she is gone from her physical body? She is still with us. You can hear her voice in this book. All who have been touched by her presence can continue that connection. It is up to each of us. We simply have to open our senses, all of our senses, and open our hearts and listen.

Love given and received is always with us.

Some details need to be mentioned. Leslye had ongoing chronic digestive issues for decades, some variety of IBS. This led to various visits to medical facilities in the US and Asia during the years leading up to her cancer diagnosis. In 2019, we were in Bali and I was scheduled to teach a course in Malaysia. We went a few days early so Leslye could get a CT Scan. The GI doctor there said she likely had Crohn's Disease but told her to go home to the States and get a Colonoscopy. She had resisted getting a colonoscopy for many years and had in fact never had one. You will read about the results of that colonoscopy, and what followed, in the following pages.

In March 2020 the whole world began to deal with the Covid19 pandemic. That intersected with Leslye's life and cancer treatments in significant ways as you will see.

One other item worthy of mention is that Leslye wanted to have a "memorial" where she could be present while she lived, not after her passing. So we did indeed hold a "Going Away Party" for her two months, almost to the day, before her passing. And what a glorious and powerful event it was!

The following pages include many emails Leslye sent out to a list of people that kept growing until the end. I've also included some personal messages. I have edited out names and personal details, as well as the names of doctors, especially when she was criticizing them.

The posting of her writings was irregular as you can see from the dates. She only wrote when she felt something bubbling up that she needed to express and the timing was unpredictable.

This is in your hands because so many folks requested a compilation of Leslye/Mukti's writing. I hope it fulfills your wishes. I hope it inspires you and that you learn something about yourself from these experiences that were so articulately shared with us all. What a gift she left us all!

What follows this introduction are Leslye's words, and any poems or quotes are ones she had chosen to accompany her writing.

- Steve

We're in a freefall into the future.
We don't know where we're going.
Things are changing so fast, and
always when you're going through
a long tunnel, anxiety comes along.
And all you have to do to transform
your hell into a paradise is to turn
your fall into a voluntary act.
It's a very interesting shift of perspective
and that's all it is…
joyful participation in the sorrows
and everything changes.

— Joseph Campbell

September 6, 2019

I made it through the exhausting prep for the colonoscopy. I didn't have a lot of strength going into the purging, but I'm so glad it's over! I was definitely scared to do the procedure but kept remembering to choose strength over fear. I prayed and surrendered. I actually felt better afterwards but the next morning I realized it was the fentanyl they gave me. I still have cramping and spend a good part of my days laying in bed with a heating pad on my tummy and happily drifting off to sleep. My life is definitely impacted right now as it is hard to muster the energy to go out and get engaged with life. But sleep is what I need to heal the intestines and since that had been lacking all week, I'm giving in to it.

They took biopsies from several areas of my intestine though I think only the very end (near the junction of small and large intestine) was significantly ulcerated. He was unable to get through to the terminal ilium. I haven't received the results of the biopsies yet, but he mentioned wanting to do another CT scan, and also the possibility of needing to remove some of my intestine. So I'm in limbo at the moment as to what sort of treatment is ahead for me. In the meantime, I'm searching for a therapist and a holistic nutritionist to help me through this journey. I commit to start next week.

September 8, 2019

I wanted to let you know that I have an MRI scheduled for Tuesday.
Once I get the biopsy results and the MRI, the doctor will hopefully come up with a treatment plan. Unfortunately the treatments are pretty

intense drugs that may require me to be in San Jose (unfortunately I'm with kaiser and their hospital and treatments for this are there) since they are IV drips or other injections. Side effects need to be monitored. Ugh...not looking forward to that!

The other outcome mentioned by the doctor is surgery to remove damaged tissue. If that is the case, I'm pretty sure I'm not going to be quickly available for much activity right away. I should know more by the end of this week,

September 13, 2019

Today I finally met with the GI doc who I met the first time last week when he primarily got more time with my butt than my face....I really like him. he is compassionate and always answers my 100's of questions.

The biopsy report shows I have a more rare colon cancer (of course! nothing in my body presents within the norms :-))

One of the things that is showing in the pathology of the tumor are cells from the stomach. Hence, I need to get the feared endoscopy. I told my doctor my fear because of the story you mentioned about a relative of yours who died getting one of them. I asked him if someone would be watching that I didn't aspirate....

I have to do the anesthesia because if I was as awake as I was with the colonoscopy, I would probably hit the doctor or involuntarily pull the tube out of my throat and tear up my esophagus. So as much as I fear getting put to sleep, I fear things down my throat more. I will just pray that nothing bad happens...and I know it's rare, and I know things happen. My friend went in for a procedure because he had a benign tumor on his pituitary gland that was beginning to affect his vision. There was a 1% chance of something going wrong...and unfortunately, he was in that 1 %...they hit an artery because it was sort of wrapped around the tumor.

This has been a huge lesson in letting go and trusting those who I really don't trust. I have had a CT scan with dye, an MRI with drinking barium, getting something injected to make my intestines slow down and getting more dye injected this week....so many scary things to surrender to.

I've been thinking about a lot of things including preparing for death. It's not that I don't have faith that I can beat this, but because it may also be in my stomach, because i'm going to need a big surgery...it is something I have to also include in my life right now. Probably something we all need to do at one time or another, but now I feel the need to get it done sooner.

I have my ups and downs....but the good news is all my blood work looks good. My liver is clean which means it hasn't gone there (so probably not a stage 4), my cancer marker blood test was low....so it's just the puzzle of the kind of tumor cell markers they see which indicate gastric cancer. And honestly, the pain I had longer than the one in my lower right area is the one area you worked on me...near the stomach. Right now, the soonest I can get the endoscopy is 25th of sept. The doctor is trying to get me in earlier but they are limited when they put people out.

I pretty much sleep a lot. and stay home.. mostly because the tumor is what has caused this partial blockage and therefore I can't eat much. sometimes a liquid diet for days and days. However, lately I've been making acorn squash boiled and mushy...and cream of rice with my homemade cashew milk...and delicious almond milk/coconut ice cream. I even ate some saltines (the first solid and crunchy thing in a month) with some cashew cheese. I had reached a new low of 91 pounds and need to gain weight and be strong for the surgery. It's an open surgery so I really need enough strength in my body to get through it. My daughter got me a more natural meal replacement than ensure...high calorie. the doctor wants me to have small frequent meals so I don't develop a complete blockage...it hurts enough as it is for things moving through the almost non existent valve from small to large intestine.

September 20, 2019

Hello all,
By now you may have heard, but if not, the illness I've been dealing with turns out to be cancer, not Crohn's disease. I am still in the testing phase since the cells in the tumor were unusual and could indicate cancer elsewhere in my body. Hopefully by the end of next week, I'll have more information.
In peace,
Leslye/Mukti

October 2, 2019

The biopsies taken from inside my stomach are clear! No cancer in there despite the pain I have in the exact same area. It was a big relief to have those biopsies confirm what the doctor saw.
Next step is interviewing a few surgeons. I want to feel at complete ease with the person cutting deep into my abdomen and removing and reconnecting my intestine.

I am doing a lot of work trying to keep my anxiety and fear at bay....to think beyond the recovery time to the time when life becomes normal again and I can be free of pain. It's been quite a journey living with the ever increasing pain. I look back in my journal and see the comments I was making months before I came to Bali about this mysterious yet constant pain. I even wrote about possibly canceling or postponing my trip to Bali due to the extreme fatigue and strange pain. I'm doing guided visualizations, support groups, personal therapy, and tomorrow I go to the first appointment to help me with my lifelong trauma.

I've been increasing the food intake but I suffer from that. Liquids are certainly easier in my system, but I desire real food sometimes. Of course, my "real food" consists of very low fiber (read white bread, white saltine crackers, white well cooked rice, etc) foods, low protein intake (too much at once hurts my tummy), low fat intake (I ate an egg today and seemed to do well with it though).

I'm trying to get out for walks because I spend too much time in bed. Besides losing weight, I've lost my strength and stamina. So even if I feel tired, I'm trying to walk every day. I love going to the beach, breathing the salty ocean air, listening to the waves and seagulls, watching the moon grow brighter after the sun sets, seeing stars appear. It's healing to me there.

I look at this world through different eyes these days. Not that I've given up hope for healing, but I'm seeing this world and my passing place in it. Getting used to the fact that I will not be here one day...and that day could be near or far, but I'm seeing how life goes on, the sun rises, daily activity begins, the sun sets, things wind down, and people come and go. Concerts will still happen, my family will continue to grow, hopefully the future generations will live on an earth that has been spared quick demise and eventual destruction...and all this continues with or without me. It's an odd, sad, yet somewhat of a peaceful way to look at things. I hope that will help my attachment issues when it's my time to go..to walk through a new door, to transition to unknown or deeply forgotten places. And preparing to do this alone...as I've always known this is the case. As you know, I lean on many in order to not do things alone. So I've been learning what it's like to walk this path on my own...albeit surrounded by the light and love of many...but ultimately alone (though I can't deny the prayers, love and healing thoughts fortify me to withstand all these scary procedures and tests and pokings and proddings).

October 4, 2019

Yes, it is my negative thinking. I think sometimes the constant pain, the lack of sleep, lack of food, all the tests, the anxiety of waiting for results, the fear of surgery, the mystery of it all...it sometimes gets to my easily available negative attitude.
We met a surgeon yesterday.we really liked her. She answered so many of our questions before we even asked them. And because of the rare and apparently aggressive cancer I have, she is going to a round table of sorts...a tumor board...to get more heads involved in this before proceeding. I liked her and felt at ease right there in the office. I think it was reflected deep within me as I slept through the night last night....first time I slept 7 straight hours in a long time!
I've started therapy with two different people...one is a meditation teacher I respect and love so

much. We're working on self forgiveness. The other is a woman who does EMDR for PTSD. I'll see how that goes...but hopefully that will help pull the roots out of my catastrophic thinking. I'm also working on writing exactly how I envision the post surgery...I get up and move soon afterwards, my body is strong and heals with no complications, walking speeds my recovery, I come home and heal quickly because my cells are strong and healthy, I surrounded by loving supported people both on this physical plane and the spiritual one, my grandchildren come visit and I am able to take them to the beach, the parks, the woods, we go camping, I attend my son's new book release party, etc....I'm going to focus on this daily and add to it. I am surrendering to the medical world and trusting they want the best outcome for me too, and I do have an incredible support system...a great nutritionist, you (very important to me), my family, my ancestors, friends, spiritual teacher. I just forget this sometimes when I'm exhausted, undernourished (still can't get my weight up to 92 pounds but keeping it above the 80's), read bad things, have pain, etc.

October 13, 2019

I am still floating in all the love and positive thoughts sent my way yesterday. I am surrounded by beautiful flowers, various stones, statues, cards, poems, and more which bring me back to the magical place we all created yesterday.
I want to thank each and every one of you for coming to be with me, for supporting my journey into trust in ways I've never known how, for giving me strength, for helping me recognize the strength in my own self once I can get rid of the obstacles to seeing that, for helping me know that you all and all those who have passed to another place

are here with me, surrounding me, teaching me, and will guide me safely wherever I need to go. You all have made me feel very loved. You have also said things that made me realize the love I feel for all of you is felt. My dirty dark little secret (won't be a secret in 1 second) is that I am both unlovable (if you REALLY knew who I was), and unable to truly love. However, I do care so deeply for all of you and trust in your words that you have felt that. I am sort of an introvert, I'm shy, I lack self confidence, I'm sometimes awkward in difficult situations.... but I am sensitive, I do feel great love for you...I care deeply about my interactions, I don't intentionally try to hurt anyone, I enjoy being with everyone (and am glad that even if years go by without seeing some of you, our connection is cemented...and it's like we've always been hanging out with each other).

I feel so blessed!!! Thank you for being a part of my life.

October 27, 2019

Hi all...Just a quick update.
It's the third day post-op. I've been healing well. No complications during surgery, and so far, except for a dip in my sodium that has been resolved, and the inability to pass gas regularly, creating pain and a distended belly, everything is going well.

It was hard managing the pain as I'm not used to the method needed and probably wait too long before I ask for pain meds.

However, last night I was moved to a new floor and might have hit the jackpot. My amazing surgeon helped me work out a pain management plan yesterday. The nurse I was assigned when I moved knows how to help surgery patients feel good! The second I mentioned pain, she was on it.

She gave me the dose I was recommended instead of half of it (which was what the other nurse had given me earlier). When that kicked in, my pain went down to ZERO!!!! I never thought I would reach zero!!! I finally knew what pain management was all about. Give a high dose that stays in the system, then give one booster of smaller dose 6 hours later. Then we'll give another high dose later, if needed while in between ill take Tylenol and ibuprofen. This will get me off the IV pain killer, and once I can eat again (eat food??? I don't know what that's like anymore), I can go home!!

The pain was so managed last night that the nurse was able to change my IV site three times (I have small beat up veins and the IV potassium is not a painless passage through these veins) and give me my nightly shot of blood thinner in my belly (usually a painful thing as the med loudly makes its way through my system) without much pain in those local sites. The nurse was amazing, treating me like her only patient in the hospital. She stayed in the room with us for over an hour as my veins did weird things with the IV and just made sure all was going perfectly before leaving us to tend to others. I even had the room to myself. Quiet, dark and clean room. She told Steve to sleep on the extra bed and she wouldn't let anyone disturb us! Poor Steve who had been sleeping in a semi-recliner chair the past 3 nights. Finally a night to stretch his body and get some real rest. He's snoring away as I write this...that sweet man! Besides my medical team, and this sweet partner of mine who has always stood by my side, my kids have been an amazing support! They are giving me round the clock support! They are so dedicated to making sure I know they are here for me! My daughter, being a nurse, really took charge over my physical needs in a big way...always my advocate when it came to dealing with the nurses, often taking over their duties which freed them to help others, giving me a luxurious sponge bath, oiling my dry body, and talking me through the scary times of IV difficulties and other unknown things I've had to face. My family has sacrificed their own time to support me with their caring love. I am lucky!

And to add to that physical and emotional support my family has given to me is the love and support and prayers you all have given to me. I know this is what has gotten me this far. From the beginning of my diagnosis to now, your love, support, concern, prayers, pep talks, and more have held me in a way I never knew possible! Words cannot express the gratitude and love I feel. I have learned how to care for others now by the love and care you've shown me. I now know the power in every little expression of this support and will pass on this love that you all have so graciously and freely given to me! I'm filled and will be proactive in passing this along to others...you have taught me to step out of my fear in receiving this abundance of love and also how to step out of it in giving it back! My heart has been opened in ways I never knew possible. Thank you so very much!!!

Now my journey is to begin to pass this stubborn gas that seems to like to stay in whatever is left of my large intestines (I truly invite myself to let it go...but I'm not doing a great job of listening). And hopefully, if I can begin taking solid foods without blowing up like a balloon, I'll be able to go home and continue on this incredible healing journey. Thank you all for being here for me. It takes a village, and I feel I've got an entire country!! I love you so much!

In love, peace and eternal gratitude,
Leslye/Mukti

November 4, 2019

Hello All
Tonight is officially one week since I've been home.
One week since I left the security of the hospital,
where advice was just a push of the button away.
Where my pain meds were automatically given to
me on a schedule. Where I didn't have to navigate
putting food down a newly reconfigured digestion
tube (since I was on nothing by mouth and then
clear liquids until the night I left).
It has been both scary and freeing to be home.
But, as has been the case since I've been sick, the
safety net of your support cradles me. When I was
scared that my incision sites suddenly got lumpy
the very night I got home, Robin willingly came to
my house to look at them (thank you so much!!).
Her loving and calming energy, as well as her
experience and knowledge allowed me to sleep
well my first night back. My dear friend/sister, who
walked this path just months before me, has
generously answered the 1001 questions that
plagued my mind.
And, of course, my incredible family has bent over
backwards to care for and support
me...encouraging me, getting my pain meds in the
middle of the night, making me rest, cooking for
me, giving me many shoulders to cry on.
I know I wouldn't be where I am today without the
love, support, well wishes and prayers from you
all. It is an astounding force...something I've never
experienced in my life but has now profoundly
changed me. It's very weird...my heart is so open
with your love and support that it has attracted
more of the same from strangers. From various
people in the hospital, to customer service on the
phone, people I don't know are offering words of
encouragement and support and love!! I am
humbled by this and can't find the words to

express my gratitude. Thank you for opening your hearts to me!!

I will not know the results of the biopsies until next week. I asked my surgeon to withhold the pathology report until I meet with her. I wanted to come home from the hospital and allow all my energies to go towards healing. Cancer is a scary word, and brings a whirlwind of emotion.

Except for the physical trauma of surgery and the readjustment of getting used to the amputation of much of the intestine, I actually have more energy now than I had for the few months preceding the surgery. I'm not living with the same kind of pain, a pain I now realize drained so much from me. I see this surgery as a gift...scared as I was to have to go through it.

Anyway, enough of me talking about me. I just wanted to fill you in and to let you know how much your love and support has meant and how it has helped with the healing. I feel like superwoman!

Thank you!!!
In much love and gratitude,
Leslye/Mukti

November 6, 2019

I turned 60 this July and had asked to finally wake up to wisdom, to self confidence, to self love. I didn't expect this was how it would manifest. In the past few months I have had to learn a lot, especially trust in a medical system I stayed away from as much as possible. I feel fortunate to have a bigger circle of complementary medical practitioners to help me navigate this new world. And a family who totally supports and willingly helps me now.

November 12, 2019

Things have been challenging. I've gotten pretty depressed. My body, which was doing ok the first few days I got home, took a dive last week. Perhaps I took too long a walk. But my insides began really hurting. So much that I increased my meds to every 4 hours again, then I developed edema in my ankles and feet. Didn't even recognize them! (I gained 4 pounds of water weight in my legs). Was checked again for blood clots. There were none. Was checked for heart, liver and kidney. All was good (though we spent 6 hours in urgent care and then ER).
I cut back on the pain meds again but had been having pain in upper abdomen and a little in chest. Pressure with deep breaths. So I was taking one oxycodone a day. I didn't think that was a lot but my surgeon thinks I shouldn't need them. She ordered a CT scan to check for infection. I went reluctantly yesterday. I also had a low grade fever Now I've got insomnia. Tempted to take Ativan to sleep but will listen to a podcast and hopefully fall asleep.
I've been nervous because I have my first post op appointment with the surgeon on Wednesday and then I meet with the oncologist. I'm scared about what they might have found. I can't seem to find my positive self. I feel alone. I hate having cancer. I hate how difficult this post surgery healing is. I hate not knowing what pain is normal and which one isn't, maybe after meeting with everyone and getting a clear picture, and knowing my surgery pain will eventually be finished, I'll feel better. Anyway, I just had to rant because I'm going crazy.
I'm even doubting my surgeon knows what she's doing...my paranoid brain is trying to take control

because I feel so trapped in this disease and feel I have no free will.
I think I should see someone soon.

Anyway, it's 4 am and I've been awake since 1:45 so I'm going to listen to a podcast and hope I fall asleep.
I love you and thank you for letting me speak my mind and heart.

November 13, 2019

Hello beautiful circle of friends,

Today is 3 weeks post surgery. Just over 2 months ago, I was told I had cancer. It was a surreal day. I had just returned from an MRI because it was thought I had Crohn's disease. The phone call from the doctors office asking me to come back to San Jose that day to talk to him was puzzling and a little voice inside me said uh oh. My family and I went to a movie that night. We were all in an altered reality and thought, what the hell...let's get out of this house. The thought that I had cancer kept creeping into my head. I realized there was life before cancer and life after cancer.
Now I feel there is life before surgery and life after surgery. Before surgery, I could do things like take long walks...go to movies...clean my house. And worry about the upcoming event that, I'm my mind, I might not survive.
Now I am three weeks post surgery. I walk mostly around my block. I have made it to the farmers market twice. I spend some days never going outside. I'm still trying to find foods I can easily digest that don't cause me extreme pain. I've pretty much stopped taking pain meds but experience pain anyway...but am trying to build a tolerance. The last week has been hellish. Been to

the ER twice...both times checking for blood clots but only one of those times did I have swelling. 4 pounds of water weight in my ankles. Extreme pain in my abdominal area which had me back on a strict routine of pain meds. Extreme pain yesterday that almost had me in the ER for a third time. The surgeon says this pain is not the normal route of healing. The leg swelling is not typical without a blood clot. So we're going to keep an eye out. And while eating seems to create pain, I need to eat. I dipped under 90 pounds now and I need to gain weight, not lose more (How did I waste so much of my life criticizing myself for being too fat when I would love to see the padding back in my butt, some flesh in my cheeks, some fat in my boobs). Calories and protein will help me heal. I want to enjoy a few weeks of robust energy (ok...maybe even mild energy) before I begin chemo.

Oh yes...chemo. The cocktail I never thought I would take. Turns out I was so focused on my fear of surgery and how to survive it, I somehow buried the fact that I had cancer. And that the cancer I had was an aggressive one. I told the surgeon I didn't want my pathology report for a few weeks. But the reality that I had cancer removed from my body and that I may need more than surgery to deal with it found its way into my psyche anyway...dreams, depression, breakdowns.

Now I know. Stage 3c...just a notch under stage 4.

With aggressive signet ring cells. 14 of 22 lymph nodes affected. T4 N2 M0...so many codes I don't know.

I'm given a prescription of 6 months of chemo...twice a month, I'm to have a port put into my chest so the chemo can be given easily.

The side effects look horrible! Luckily I can get advice from women who have been through this. But I imagine this potentially life saving nectar will make me pay a price for an extended life. Oh goodness, this is not a positive way to phrase this. I will work on seeing this as a true gift. Sort of like the powerful mushroom or other strong medicine that purges the body of what it no longer needs to make way for truth or knowledge. I will try to visualize this as divine golden nectar...from the spirits who heal...to destroy the rogue cells and then hope I've gotten my base strong enough to rise like the Phoenix once I'm reduced to ashes...cancer cells not allowed to join in the rebirth,

It's late and my visualizations are getting mingled and misused. If you have any to share, I'd love to hear of them, I invite your prayers and powers of positivity and connections to the sweet divine to help me open to this new form of healing.
I read things get worse as treatments go on. The mouth and stomach cells go with the cancer cells. The white blood cells go away too making it difficult to socialize for fear of getting really sick. The nausea, the neuropathy, the cold sensitivity, the mouth sores, the fatigue.
I imagine this will be the year for hell. But it's an necessary price to pay if I become cancer free. And if some of you are interested in giving me rides for treatment and hanging out with me, please let me know. 6 months is a long time. Since I've fallen asleep several times since beginning this, I'll say good night. And I love you. And thank you for your love and support.

November 15, 2019

I have been very confused and depressed these last two days. I haven't gotten clear answers about treatment given the rare and aggressive cancer I have. I feel closed in a box with no way out. I know this may just be a normal feeling when confronting ones mortality and trying to make a decision. I have to weigh quality of life against going through hell for a chance to beat this. Will it pay off? No one can tell me. There is more testing that kaiser won't do as I'm not stage 4. Though I'm told there are two spots on my liver that are too small to know yet if they're cancer, which would make it stage 4.

I'm just lost. Perhaps it's something anyone goes through as they sort out the shitty options. And I still suffer from the surgery. And I still lose a pound a day. I just have to get some clarity. I accept that my end could be near, and in that case I want quality of life, not the hellish side effect laden life. But if I can handle it, I'd do it.

I guess the thing I need the most is strength...strength and grace and love and beauty fir whatever the outcome is. I'm just in a fucking funk right now.

I'm sorry I'm so down. A combo of healing from surgery, still in pain, faced with chemo and uncertainty, and possibility effects of all the drugs I've had, I'm in mucky waters. But the lotus blooms from the mud, right?

November 19, 2019

Insomnia is great for catching up.
Whoa, what a journey this is! I think I have let myself become too obsessed with cancer. I joined a Facebook group that's all about colon cancer...a huge community of people. While there is valuable info there, I see how easy it is to become obsessed with it...waking and looking online for info, asking questions for more info, insomnia and getting in it for hours...it's too much!
I like support and should just stick to the one in-person support group and the one online support

group with 8 people and a social worker. I'm getting overwhelmed in this world of too much info.

Ever since my pathology results came back, life has not been easy. I think I've gone into a depression and it's hard to get out. 14 lymph nodes affected with cancer. Tumor grew all the way through the colon (T4 is how they classify it). aggressive signet ring cell and mucinous cancer make my prognosis worse than just regular colon cancer. And the side effects of chemo are horrifying!!! Neuropathy, cold sensitivity that make it feel like glass in your throat...not to mention the regular nausea, low white blood count making your immune system weak...

I've been in a box with no way out...feeling damned if I do, damned if I don't. And that's not the mindset needed to go into chemo and beat this thing I called a psychiatrist yesterday and hope to see him this week. I need to get out of my funk. I need to be strong and positive and give it my best chance. Of course, I think of side effects and quality of life and wonder what to choose. But maybe if I can minimize the side effects (the chemo is very strong) by techniques others have tried...if I can see the drugs as a gift of healing...if I can learn visualizations that direct the drugs to the cancer cells and not the healthy cells... I just need to break out and get there! But I'm not feeling that yet. I'm reading Love, Medicine and Miracles and see in myself where I have t really chosen life yet. Part of it is I'm still recovering from the surgery and haven't had pain free days since stopping the meds. Maybe I should restart them. But if my body felt better now, I'd feel stronger going into chemo. So I need to work on that. Part of it is I had to stop my HRT and get hot flashes and probably mood swings. And part of it is I just want to go outside

and enjoy a hike or walk..not be immersed in being in surgeries recovery and focused on cancer.
So there you have it...me at the bottom of this struggle fighting to get out. And after I see the psych, maybe I'll be there. He does hypnotherapy too so that can help.
If I could sleep that would help too.
On the positive side, I have a great nutritionist who is fighting with me...looking for ways to mitigate the chemo with nutrients. I'm meeting with a doctor who uses IV vitamin C and maybe other things that may help. And I talked to an integrative oncologist who is encouraging...says do the chemo AND he's sending me therapies from Germany that I will inject to help my immune system. I'm hearing about fasting before chemo to help with side effects. So I am going to psyche myself up to choose life, chemo to help, and trust in my body to be strong and get through it. Of course, no guarantees this will make me free of cancer, it's just the best shot.
Ugh...

My grandchildren are here now. The days have been warm and sunny. My room is cozy. I'm not working and will be getting a small disability check (so I can catch up on the missed sleep if I can ever make myself nap). We're having major work done to our house...meaning we need a retaining wall in the back and took a loan to finally do that and save it from damage. I can eat an egg and toast without pain..but need more food to gain weight (I got to a low of 88 pounds!!!). I'm slowly getting rid of things and it feels really good. If only I could do the same with the paperwork...I seem to believe I'll need any of those 1000's of papers one day.
I'm going to explore CBD and maybe stronger things for both the pain and for sleep.

Thank you for always sending your love, your hugs, your sweet poems and quotes...I appreciate it all even if I don't get back to you in a timely manner.

I'm sure my next email will be much more positive! And I hope you love me even if this one isn't

November 24, 2019

Hello All,

First I want to say, I'm finding writing a wonderful way to connect. It's also helpful to my spirit. However, I know all the things I say are not always positive, but they are me and this is what I'm going through. I go to the depths of despair at times, and I rise to the joy of each day, or each moment.

The pain from surgery gets me down, the prospect of chemo, a horrible chemo, a debilitating to the extent I never knew kind of chemo that may give long lasting or even permanent side effects that are painful sort of chemo.

Facing my demons...digging up all those ugly things, the regrets for my mistakes, making peace with my actions or lack of actions. Seeing the beauty and love and letting it in...letting it saturate my cells, my heart, my spirit. Being awed at the loving generosity of my friends and family, at how people reach out and stand by my side with love and support. I have learned so much about how to be there because of the support of all of you. Especially the friends I have been connected to for most of my life but not in this intimate way, you reach out to my heart as if you are my sister, brother, mother, father...with such tender care and support. In my life, I had a hard time "meeting people without fear" as Babaji mentions. Now I finally get it.

Anyway, I realized I was writing to you without your permission. I know if someone writes a blog, people who want to read it subscribe. Here, I'm sending emails. Of course, you always have the choice to delete. But, I just want to know...if you don't want to get my emails, Please respond to me and I'll remove you from my list.
Otherwise, I'll be writing soon to report on all I've learned this past week...
I love you all!
xoxoxo
Leslye

December 11, 2019

Waking up at 3:30 or 4 am daily, I can either try (unsuccessfully) to go to sleep, listen to guided mediations and visualizations (this is my should do), read the various cancer forums and search for more info (this is my shouldn't do but us what I always do) or write an update. After an hour on cancer forums and emailing my oncologist to plead for more testing on my tumor, I've decided to write an update. Please forgive any spelling errors as I'm doing this on my tiny phone rather than the computer.

Why do I obsess with cancer research? One big reason is I'm facing a treatment that is very hard on the body. 90% of the people on this particular drug get neuropathy...of various degrees and almost always permanently. That's just one side effect. (If you know me, you know I rarely take any drugs because of possible side effects...I will avoid antibiotics as long as possible, I won't take cough medicine or decongestants because of side effects, etc).

But I search relentlessly because I have a rare form of colon cancer. My tumor had signet ring cells. These are aggressive and could be hard to diagnose as they line the mesenteric tissues. And because it's rare in colon cancer, the treatment protocol is standard colon cancer treatment...which I mentioned is a hard chemo that causes so many quality of life issues. But I'm told it's my chance at wiping out cancer from my body.

I now know what depression looks and feels like. I spent days in bed crying..buried under the covers. I felt boxed in...locked in a box with no way out. Hope was nowhere to be found. This is not what I wanted. And knowing I have a cancer that has so many signs of a poor prognosis... poorly differentiated, MSS, signet ring, mucinous, a lot of lymph node involvement....it makes my head spin. And the strange thing is, except for this cold/flu thing, I feel pretty good! I want to know that the treatment I must do will help ruin/destroy/ eradicate the cancer cells...will make them unable to reproduce anywhere in my body. If I must go through this chemo, it must be effective. But, the sad truth is...there are no guarantees. And with signet ring, there are less guarantees. So that is the negative side of all this. And finding medical advice about this is difficult. I've found one place in Ohio that is focusing on this form of cancer but they're just beginning.

So, here is where my faith, my prayers, and your prayers will come in. This is what will get me through the strong chemo that is going to try to kill the cancer cells. This is what will help me overcome my fears of having an aggressive cancer. This is what will help me live each day with appreciation...get me out of my head and into my heart.

I understand stress, anxiety, worry and depression will not help my body heal. I get that. I really, really, really know this from deep in my core. But guess what?!? It's one thing to intellectually know this and another to achieve eliminating it from my mind. So what can I do? I think I need to reach into my heart. I think I need to reach into my soul. I think I need to connect with the river of love, of spirit, of the eternal that we all are part of. And it's not always easy.

So, I reach out to you, my wise friends and family, for help in bringing me back to the place of inner peace. I don't need your well intentional suggestions on second or third opinions, or what herb to try or whether or not to do chemo, or this supplement or sign up for treatment at some amazing place in Mexico, or eat only this or never eat that or anything like that. I have an amazing team helping me navigate all that and it meets all my needs. What I most need is how to use the tools I have to connect to the spirit of peace and love, of acceptance...of being in this moment, right now. And this encompasses the reality of sadness. I will be sad. Anyone who has a life threatening disease that has brought death closer to their door will be sad...I mean, we all want to live, right? Even though we know we will die. And those of us with aggressive cancer face the reality of death daily. I look around when I go to the bakery with my family and wonder how many times will I do this again. I watch life go on and know I may not be part of this dance of life in the near future. It's a reality for all of us, right? By doing this, I'm not conceding to this disease...believe me! But it is something I imagine anyone with a life threatening disease thinks about more than the average person. Impermanence. Those on a spiritual path think about this from time to time. "I am not my body. This world is an illusion. God is you and you are God." Perhaps this is my opportunity to find that truth we often read about and practice for. So I need this live connection that you all have been so generously giving me. Bringing me back, again and again to my heart. To my peace. To our peace. I hope this is a symbiotic thing...because I want to give back to you all you give to me. I want the love to burn fiercely in your heart too. I want the peace you bring to me bring you peace too. I wish this for all of us.

Yesterday I went with my son and grandkids to natural bridges. We lay on the ground watching the butterflies flutter above us...orange wings against the blue sky. The scent of the earth, rich from the rains and the sun, the fragrant eucalyptus trees, the silence, the buzzing of bees..there we lay, in that moment, immersed in life around us. Special times. There is something wonderful about being out in the natural world, silent, being present in the moment with what is.

On the practical side, I am getting an MRI today to see if the spots found in my liver on a CT scan in November are gone or not. If these were bruising from surgery, they will be gone. I suppose they could be a multitude of things...and we're hoping they are not cancer. In September nothing was seen. But I believe I've had spots on my liver in the past...and they were nothing.

My treatment will remain the same even if they are cancer...I will start chemo (on New Year's Eve!!! Yay for the biggest cocktail I've ever had) and then have surgery on my liver if needed after chemo. I think this is the new life with advanced and aggressive cancer...chemo, surgery, CT scans, MRI, time off treatment, more treatment, more scans, repeat. I will adjust to this new norm as long as I get my moments to be in nature, to hear the water trickle in the creek, the hear sings of birds and insects, to smell the rich earth, to see the green of the trees...to be with people I love, to sing (off key as usual for me) and dance (don't laugh) and walk on the beach. To see the rainbows, the hear the raindrops, to feel my breath enter and leave my body, right here, right now.

I have a great team of helpers outside of traditional treatment. My amazing nutritionist friend who has been on my team from the minute I was misdiagnosed with Crohn's disease. Not only does she give me supplements and nourishing foods, she calms my spirit when I get out there. She brings me back to a place of peace. I was gifted a visit with an integrative oncologist by a lifelong friend, through him, I'm being treated with mistletoe and other organ supporting supplements. His goal is to strengthen my body and fight the cancer with these so the chemo works better. Through another lifelong friend, I have been connected with an advocate doctor, helping us navigate this cancer journey. He has been an invaluable source of information as well as soothing my soul and spirit with his Sufi training...something dear to my heart. I have a great psychiatrist who records visualizations to get me through these tough times. My primary care physician has been my advocate through the kaiser system. She regularly calms me to check in. I have never felt so cared for by a "regular" doctor. I recently connected with Steve's long time family doctor. She is helping with my alternative treatments too (Mistletoe injections). I have a medical Qi gong/Chinese medicine practitioner. Being in his office, with the calming crystals, and his competent energy, has been amazing. He is a true healer! I have a meditation teacher who is a lifeline for bringing me back to acceptance and peace. He is teaching me that I am lovable. I am imperfectly perfect. I am worthy of self forgiveness. I feel such peace in his presence. It is a gift. And of course, all of you.

I hear often you know who your friends are when you get cancer. I think I'm the luckiest person in the world. All of you have been so loving and present with me through all of this. You've helped me get through every scary step I've taken. Your inspiring words, your prayers, your visions of competent surgeons and successful procedures, your texts, your calls, the photos of your gardens or beautiful places in nature, your visits, the food, the jokes, the songs, the walks, the rides I need...the list goes on and on. Mere words cannot express the gratitude I feel, the love I feel, the happiness I feel. You have helped me open my heart like it's never been before. Some say cancer is a turning point. I get it now..you have helped heal my long held wounds that prevented me from feeling worthy of receiving love. Those barriers I created to protect myself were not strong enough to stop the outpouring of love. Love wins!

And finally, I don't know how or why, as I certainly have been a challenge to live with, but my family has shown up with the utmost of support and love...above and beyond anything I've ever imagined. They are by my side through the tears and fears. They give me strength when I don't think I have another drop left. I'm not an easy person, and yet they show up through it all. I am blessed to have such an amazing family. The ones I live with and my extended family...all loving and supporting me and each other. My beautiful and strong ancestors...loving and supporting me and supporting my family. Love is powerful.

Thank you all for loving me!

I love you all very very very much! xoxoxox

January 2, 2020

Good bye 2019! You did not deliver the awakening I was expecting! But you did profoundly affect me and my family.

There have been experiences in our lives that have done this....losses of loved ones that hit so hard you wonder how life can keep going on each day when you are stuck in some kind of limbo.

Or, the birth of your first child. Nothing can prepare you (or at least, nothing prepared me) for the complete change that happens once that baby comes into this world. I remember it being like a brand new set on a stage...the curtain to the old set closed and reopened to a completely different scene...that's what having your first child is like.

Getting a cancer diagnosis, at least for me and my immediate family, had that same effect. Those words you never want to hear after a doctor appointment. I still remember how stunned we were from the news, tears falling, hugs, tears, collapsing in a daze, more tears, numbness...and then we decided to go to the movies. It was surreal...getting in the car, sitting in the theater. Crying in the theater. Trying to get lost in the movie while the thought, "I have cancer" kept coming back into my head. We all were like zombies moving through the world...in the world but not really part of it.

Many scary procedures behind me now, successful in large part because of all the love and support I have received from my family and you, my community of amazing friends, I now face another journey I never wanted to take...chemotherapy.

Chemotherapy....chemotherapy. I keep writing the word because in my mind, it has been my enemy. Now I have to befriend this powerful poison, this drug that has the potential to kill any cancer cells that are floating in my body. I need to see it as healing juice. The problem is...I don't. Yet, I need to! So, I work with visualizations, recordings made for me to reframe this, and therapy.

There is one drug I'm particularly afraid of....Oxaliplatin. Ox-alley-platin. When my oncologist says the name of if, it sounds to me like a word you would use to play hand clapping games to in kindergarten. Ox (clap) alley (clap) platin (double clap). Or maybe jump rope to the sing song-y sound...*Ox, ox alley platin. Ox alley platin came out to play, on a bright and sunny day.*

This drug has horrible side effects (which chemo drug doesn't?) There are things people do to try to avoid these side effects. They are painful, but not as painful as the damage it causes. So, people suggest icing your hands and feet the entire time of infusion (2 hours!!!). Yup, keep your hands and feet on ice so you can hopefully close up the capillaries so the chemo cannot go there. And keep ice in your mouth the entire time...even though you may feel the razor blades going down your throat. I don't know if I can do that....I'm going to need a lot of encouragement from those who have done this in order for me to be brave enough to do it. I'm going to try my hardest so I can avoid these side effects. There are a lot of kick ass folks out there getting this drug, having side effects, and moving forward with strength and a positive attitude because it is going to keep them free of cancer! Because the tumor I had was aggressive and unusual, I will join this group of warriors. I will go through hell and come out the other side. I'm definitely going to need all the prayers and support for this journey. I had a vision of the Goddess Kali manifesting in my body...the chemo transformed into Kali...with her fierce warrior strength, attacking the cancer cells, transforming them into pure cells once again, giving the rest of my body the courage it needs to withstand the intense cleansing, to have faith in this journey of transformation.

One night when I woke at 3 am and was on my relentless search for information, I said, enough! I searched instead for positive quotes on beating cancer. I saw something by Eve Ensler. She has been a hero of mine for decades with the work she does for women worldwide. She is also a survivor of sexual abuse (her father) and a painful childhood. I checked out her book, *The Body of the World* from the library. It's a memoir which includes her journey with cancer. Reading it, I identified with her in many ways. She had fears of not surviving surgery too. She couldn't stand the thought of chemo. I want to write a couple of passages here that helped me feel I could handle the chemo. She was talking to her friend/therapist about not being able to face doing chemo, among other things. This is what her friend told her:

The chemo is not for you. It is for the cancer, for all the past crimes, it's for your father, it's for the rapists, it's for the perpetrators. You're going to poison them now and they are never coming back. Chemo will purge the badness that was projected

41

onto you but was never yours. I have total faith in your resilience and the magical capacities of your body and soul for healing. Your job is to welcome the chemo as an empathetic warrior, who is coming in to rescue your innocence by killing off the perpetrator who got inside you. You have many bodies; new ones will be born out of this transformational time of love and care. When you feel nauseous or terrible, just imagine how hard the chemo is fighting on your behalf and on the behalf of all women's bodies, restoring wholeness, innocence, peace. Welcome the chemo as empathetic warrior.

Ride the lion with all the strength and love that you have found in your community. Although this anguish is very lonely, there is a new infant being born, in a community of love, protection, tenderness, and ferocious caregiving. We are all around you with our blessings. You are here with me. The live force in you is being released. Kali is being purged from your cells, so that your cells run clean of cancer, and your selves run clean of the projected not-you badness that has riddled you all of your life. Washed clean, you are finding your original goodness.

I didn't want to get cancer so that I could finally get rid of the "projected not-you badness that has riddled you all of your life." Nor did I want it to help me find my original goodness. However, this journey has been an awakening to all this. I am being born into "a community of love, protection, tenderness and ferocious caregiving" because of you all! I am surrounded by your love and blessings. And believe me, I feel it! I only hope you feel back the fierce love I have for you, that you feel my gratitude for your love. I am blown away by the capacity of giving, of loving and of support you have given me on this journey of uncertainty. It means so much to me, and very importantly, it means so much to my family. Your love and support has touched my kids and grandchildren so deeply. I know it is healing for them to witness such love and support. I can't thank you enough! I love you all so much!

Thank you for being here with me. I send blessings and love to all of you too. I hope you feel this big wave of love coming your way.

xoxoxox

Mukti/Leslye

January 8, 2020

Hello beautiful community,

Steve pointed out my last email didn't really give an update on what's been happening...and believe me, it's been a lot! I haven't had a week go by without some appointment or another.

I postponed chemo until next week (1/15). As I mentioned, I've had a hard time accepting it. I listen to a visualization recording from a friend of mine, I cry, I re-read Eve Ensler's words, I look at images of goddesses, I pray...and I still feel shaky, scared, depressed about it. When I think about it making me weak and sick, I think of the women in my support group. They are resilient. They come to the group while on chemo. They are living, working, walking, going out....so this is what I have to remember.

Tomorrow I get the port surgery. I'm nervous about this. Not only the procedure itself, but the symbol of it, the meaning of it. One step closer to chemo. For those of you who don't know what a port is (i'd never heard of one myself until recently), it's some device they implant in the chest. It has a tube or something that goes directly into an artery so the chemo won't blow out the veins. It lives there for the six months...or, really a year (they want to leave it in for future use...not too encouraging, eh??). I'd rather be sipping port...a delicious port spreading warmth through my body. Why can't that abolish any cancer?

I met a new oncologist yesterday in SF. He was recommended because he (supposedly) is open to non invasive testing of the tumor, which is something I've been trying to get done. I have discovered not one oncologist will test the tumor (from stored tissue after the surgery). I wanted it tested for mutations and such, but it seems they only do that with stage 4 tumors so people can be directed to other treatment plans....biologics, other targeted therapies, immunotherapy, clinical trials, etc. He didn't support my desire for this. At least I can say I tried. And, really, I haven't stopped. But I'm kind of tired of doing this right now and am going to give it a rest. Thank goodness I have an oncologist here who will treat me with lower dose chemotherapy. With the mistletoe and glandular support, I should do really well.

I have been doing so many other forms of building my body, and hopefully destroying (someone told me I shouldn't see it like that, but should think transforming) any cancer floating in my body so the chemo has allies. Wow, I just married the botanicals with the drug....may I continue to see it like that. I guess I've really been looking at the chemo as a cancer itself! This is why writing is so healing...it helps expose the way I understand things. So, chemo is an ally in fighting cancer, not another cancer to fight. The doctors tell me this is going to help make cancer a thing of the past. I know they like to believe that...they have to believe that...because this is what they do. And they see success a lot of the time. If they didn't, I would imagine their hearts would not allow them to continue doing this. My oncologist here in Santa Cruz has a good heart. She believes she's helping me.

My amazing nutritionist, besides helping me manage all the supplements I need without spending the entire day taking them (I do spend a good 3 hours a day getting it all in) and advising me on foods to help my body, has gotten my "case" in with a group of amazing herbalists, nutritionists and doctors. Collectively, they have over 50 years of working with people with cancer so I feel I'm in good hands.

I am also working with a medical Qi gong teacher who has worked with cancer patients. Besides the Qi gong, he formulated a Chinese herb powder for me. He has taught me to do breathing exercises (different than those I practice to calm the mind) that alkalinize and oxygenate the body...two things cancer cells do not like. It is a method taught by Wim Hof, and it includes getting in cold water. I've tried that in the shower...trying to overcome the feelings of being cold, losing my breath, etc. It is not easy but i'm telling myself I am not my body....I think the push to challenge my comfort level is stronger now because I will definitely be pushing it with all the procedures. Look him up if you want to do some interesting breath work.

I have been getting out hiking again. I notice my legs are not as strong as they were, but it feels soooo good to be outside. I've gone with my family to Land of the Medicine Buddha, various trails at Wilder Ranch State Park, walking along the beach, and walking the hill behind soquel high again. I love it! I'd love to walk with YOU! Especially during chemo treatment. I think I'll need the extra nudge to get out so please feel free to ask me...or drag me outside.

Scanxiety....a new word I learned from my cancer groups. It is real. Every time I've had to get an MRI, or CT, I observed myself being sort of grumpy the day before. I now know it's because I'm scared of what the results will be.

I'll be having a new test...a PET scan. It's like a CT scan but I'll have the added pleasure of some radioactive glucose injected inside my body. Cancer is more metabolically active than regular cells...and it likes glucose. So the radioactive glucose travels to and lights up on the scan where there is more activity. Because I have a lymph node in my neck that is big enough to cause swelling in my neck, we're checking. It may also show activity other places....like those too small spots on my liver that most likely are not cancer. Or anywhere else in my body cancer may be lurking. It is my hope there is NO cancer lurking anywhere in my body and the lymph node is swollen from something else. But there is always the fear in the back of my mind when things are not like they should be. I ignored a colonoscopy and ended up with a very big tumor. I don't want to ignore other symptoms, but I don't want to get caught up in the cycle of tests and fear. There has to be a balance here.

Despite all these scary things going on, my life feels blessed! I have the best family one could every hope for. I am blessed with so many caring friends. My team of practitioners have enlightened and guided me in ways I would never have thought. Besides the ever present Grace and Love of my Teacher, I have many spiritual guides who are helping me deal with my life long issues so I may have peace in my daily life.

Thank you for all the rides, for bringing music to my house and heart, for the delicious and nourishing meals, for the tickets to shows where we can dance and let the music heal us, for the texts or emails sending your thoughts or poems or love, for the walks, for the books, for the pictures, for the cards, for the phone calls, for the visits, for the flowers. Thank you for your love, for your support, for your prayers. Thank you for letting me cry in your arms, for making me laugh, for helping me know I have a community of caring and loving people in my life. I hope you all feel my immense love going out toward you. I feel that love moving into each of us...as if we're in a big circle, arms around each other, the love traveling like energy into and around all of us. I just couldn't do this without you! You are my nutrition and you keep me going strong!

Please think some positive thoughts for an easy surgery Thursday....and a speedy recovery. I want to be strong going into chemo and want the port surgery site to heal quickly. I'll mentally be holding hands with you....

Much love always!
xoxoxox
Mukti/leslye

January 21, 2020

I wanted to let you know how your singing prayers helped me last week.
I'd awakened at 4am in tears, not wanting to go to chemotherapy. I wrote you. Around 6:45 am I had more strength to do it. I know I needed to do it but

something had shifted inside. I know your prayers helped me.
Thank you!!!!
I love you.

I've got 11 more treatments to go. I also have some testing I'm on the fence about...namely a PET scan. One doctor says it lights up a lot of things and would create questions and uncertainties. I think we'll go fir the needle biopsy instead...since the node in my neck is still big. My acupuncturist (he's really more of a healer of many modalities) told me to put castor oil pack on it and envision it shrinking. He said even if it's cancer, do it.
This is a journey of uncertainty. Learning to live in this way, especially for me, a person with so little trust, is hard. But I can't have life be hard really...because I have to learn to love each moment...each darn uncertain moment.
I certainly love you!

January 28, 2020

Hello Dear Friends
Today my son Nathan, daughter-in-love Sari, and my two grandchildren Nasya and Maxwell went back to Bali where they live. It is a sad day for me. It's actually been a sad week. They have been staying here in my house and now it is disturbingly quiet and empty, even though 4 of us live here and Kusum is here every day.
I know they have a life there, school for the kids, business to get back to....I just selfishly want them here with me....all the time. So if this email sounds dark and depressing, it's because i'm grieving. I'm sure it doesn't help to go into treatment feeling so sad

I'm not feeling very creative so this is more of a "keeping you updated with boring details" kind of email.

When I met with my oncologist, we discussed increasing the dose of the chemotherapy drugs I'm getting. My first treatment was very low dose. I'm too scared to increase the oxaliplatin, but will allow an increase in the 5FU, which I hear is the bigger fighter of cancer anyway. Last treatment, I took valium before I went. That helped me relax and has made the memory of that day somewhat vague. I iced my hands and feet the entire 3 hours (taking short breaks) to help with side effects. Tomorrow, along with icing my hands and feet, I'll keep ice in my mouth and wrap a cold pack around my throat. It's supposed to help with the side effects that happen in the throat. The nurses were supportive of my icing last time (although it was discouraged when I first mentioned it) so hopefully they will support the ice in the mouth. If this works to minimize or prevent the horrible side effects, it could create an icing protocol that will help others who get platinum drugs not get the permanent neuropathy.

I think one of the hardest things I've been dealing with is UNCERTAINTY. We all face uncertainty. What is difficult for me is the question, will this chemotherapy work. How will I know if it's working. There is nothing to really measure that right now. Will it do more harm if I increase the dosage? Will it be enough if I don't? This is where I must rely on faith. I've never really been good with trust and faith. It's a stretch for me. What I'm learning is we only have this moment. This moment, here on this earth, in this body, with a community of others whom I love and who love me. I have this day, this hour, this minute....to love and appreciate. Yet the time is also spent with sadness, with frustration, stabbing my body, hijacking my mind. It's not something I can control right now. It is something I can distract myself from though. I can feel when I'm not really present. It's a weird thing...when I'm out in the world where there are a lot of people (like the boardwalk, where I took my grandchildren recently), I observe people like I never did before. I look at the grandpa walking with his toddling 2 year old granddaughter to the carousel. I see young couples with babies, just starting their families. I imagine their lives, their healthy bodies, carefree in a way I don't know if i'll ever be again. Having a spiritual practice (though there have been definite gaps in the practice), I get this life, this body, is just an illusion (though it feels like the end all be all). I know we all will die. It's just weird when you have a disease that brings the reality of that end a little closer....and when you are surrendered to a world of medicine you never thought you'd be part of. I'm sure there is a lot to be learned, and I hope I'm learning it quickly. I am learning it's okay to be sad and depressed and that doesn't minimize the joy and happiness and gratitude I also feel.

Am I being too dark? I apologize. Blame it on the day. It's always a sad day when my family goes back to Bali. I guess this is the lesson in acceptance and letting go.

I read the following in an article about Alex Trebek, the host of game show Jeopardy, who is dealing with stage 4 pancreatic cancer:

In a preview of the profile on "Good Morning America" on Wednesday, People Magazine shared that Trebek believes his support system could have contributed to the positive turnaround to his health. He said his doctors agree.

"I told the doctors, this has to be more than just chemo," Trebek said. "I've had a couple million people out there who have expressed their good thoughts, their positive energy and their prayers. The doctors said it could very well be an important part of this."

I feel the same about all of you. The amazing love and positive energy you send my way definitely carries me through all this. Wherever this journey leads me, I know I am surrounded by love so strong. I bring the image of all this love with me all the time. I bring it to the OR, to the infusion center, I think about it when I'm sad and confused. Thank you so much, from the depth of my being, for all the love and good thoughts.

Tomorrow I go to treatment #2. I will be bringing all your love and good wishes with me, and will return home, knowing I'm still bathed in that power.
Thank you, thank you, thank you.
Peace, love and beauty to all of us.
xoxoxoxox
Leslye/Mukti

February 12, 2020

Hi All
It's been a rough week or so. If you prefer to read more upbeat updates, you might want to delete this.

I'm learning it's okay to have some rough times, some depressed times, some "I can't believe this is my life" moments. Those feelings are part of the whole picture and I'm not a failure if I experience the spectrum of human emotions.

Given all I've learned these past few months, given that I've experienced more love than I ever allowed into my life in the past, given that I want to value the moment and not get bothered by the small stuff, it bothers me that I'm not the person I want to be yet. I don't want to get bothered if the door is left open....again. I don't want to look at my sweetie and begin to doubt his love for me because life has taken a huge turn and suddenly I need him by my side more than ever. I don't want to feel I'm sucking all the energy out of anyone. Sometimes I sink into doubt.

I am so lifted and amazed by all the love sent my way, by the devoted caring I'm receiving from my children, the delicious meals you bring, the music and singing circles, by the great fortune to have so many people on my "team" who are helping me get through this, guiding me through the jungle of traps, and a loud voice screams out to me: YOU DON'T DESERVE THIS!

Your task is not to seek for love, but merely to seek and find all the barriers within yourself that you have built against it. — Rumi

I try to remember that quote. Keep pushing the barriers I built away. I guess I'm still finding more barriers.

It's been rough because yesterday, Feb 10, was the 15th anniversary of my mom's death. I can't believe 15 years have gone by without her phone calls, without her practical jokes, without her visits, without her cuteness in her visors, shorts, sneakers, and a fanny pack. I loved her sense of adventure. I loved how much she loved her grandchildren. In fact, they probably received more pure love from her when they were growing up than came from me. That's how much she loved them. She was way too young (67) to die from leukemia. I mourn because I was not by her side at the moment of her death. I was on the phone and my lovely sister held the phone to her ear moments before she passed so I could talk to her (she was pretty unconscious by that time). I spent 6 weeks with her once she was sent home to hospice. Selfishly, I wanted to rent an RV and bring her home to Santa Cruz with me. I wanted to nurture her and see if we could beautify her remaining days. I liked hospice in Santa Cruz way better than hospice in Hollywood, Florida.

I did find someone to come and sing sweet songs to her and I saw how it comforted her. I wanted to give her all kinds of sweet comfort. Unfortunately, it seems when death is sort of near, family members can't always join forces. I'm sure there are families who bond and support each other in ways that support the precious dying person. I've seen families come apart when someone is dying. Perhaps that person was the uniting force and the others really have nothing to do with each other. The peacemaker is not in charge. That was my mom. Full of love, loving each person in her family, bringing everyone together. I love her so much and miss her tremendously. So I think this hitting after a bad week was just too much. And I'm fragile sometimes. More than I know. I'm trying to give myself the space to be the sad, depressed, fragile person I am as well. I know the love still exists...it didn't run away.

Your task is not to seek for love, but merely to seek and find all the barriers within yourself that you have built against it. — Rumi

This week is chemotherapy week #3. Time to prepare my broth and almond milk. Today I was taking the skin off the soaking almonds. Thankfully this batch of almonds has skin that easily slips off when I squeeze the almonds in my fingers.

During my last treatment, I began to feel a little dizzy for a minute. I mentioned that to the nurses and they sort of scolded me for fasting. But fasting has so far helped me not get nauseous. Well, that and the antinausea meds they put in the IV line on Wednesday and Friday.

I'm going to need a little extra love from you all tomorrow. Because of the sadness I've been stuck in and because of the physical pain I've had for the past week and the emotional stress that created, I'm not going to my treatment with the full positive force I like to manifest inside myself.

So, if you don't mind thinking and sending some extra strong healing thoughts my way, seeing my body as strong, seeing the chemotherapy entering my body to do the job of scouting for and eliminating cancer cells and leaving my healthy cells alone as much as possible, seeing my nerve pathways protected by the ice on my hands and feet and mouth and throat...doors closed to side effects. I know you have your own visions of how to send strength to my body (minus any cancer cells, which are part of my body but i'm kicking them out) so I'm just gonna clear the obstacles I might have in receiving that and feel all this coming at me, entering me, accompanying me, surrounding me. The beautiful energy of love, love, love.

I am humbled and honored by all this love. Thank you, thank you, thank you. I couldn't do this journey without your love and support.

See you on the other end (you see, I sleep for 12-15 hours a day after chemotherapy) and hopefully my brain will land back in my head so I can write again sooner.

xoxoxoxoxoxoxoxoxoxoxoxoxoxoxoxoxoxo
JaiGurudev,

Love,
Leslye/Mukti
(I've been thinking about this name of mine, Mukti, recently....it means *liberation*)

February 13, 2020

Hello Dear Ones

I had my treatment yesterday. So far so good. I have the pump attached, giving me chemotherapy until tomorrow. I'm told each treatment gets a little worse with side effects as the toxins build up. Hopefully with all the extra herbal and nutritional support I'm getting, I'm building my body to be strong and handle this.
I take my altar with me, I listen to the healing mantra for some of the time, and I slept for a little when I was getting the pre meds (the valium makes me brave and sleepy).
It's hard to sleep when I'm getting ice shoveled into my mouth continuously :-) (thank you Steve and Cathy for feeding me ice for 2.5 hours) so during the oxaliplatin infusion, I stay awake (though that is when I imagine the chemotherapy going where it needs to go).

I've been negotiating with my oncologist for lower dose of one of the chemotherapy agents...the one that damages the nerves and causes electric shocks in the jaw, and possible permanent peripheral neuropathy....hence the icing of hands, feet and throat. She reluctantly is going along with my request. Which is why I allowed 100% of the other chemotherapy agent, and this time an iron infusion. My iron has dropped a lot so when she told me it's pretty innocuous, I said okay. I feel I need to choose my "battles" so to speak.

Emotionally, I'm feeling better. I think I can thank the valium for that. It was such a hard week and the day before my chemotherapy I discovered I might have created a hernia from doing a very intense session of Qi gong (did I already mention this? My mind is not clear). I had pain and swelling in my groin. Of course my first thought was, uh oh, cancer. That is the sucky thing about having cancer. Swollen lymph nodes, pencil thin poop (with colon cancer, we talk about poop a lot), headaches...you name it, and I'll think cancer is showing up. I don't want to think like that, and it happens. I'll be getting it checked out to see if it's a pulled muscle, a hernia or, as my surgeon mentioned, a blood clot. Good to rule these things out.

As fate would have it, I received a call from a friend/psychiatrist that I've been seeing to help me along this path. I told him he's psychic because I was going to call him to schedule an appointment after having such a bad week. I guess we're really all connected.

I've been blessed on this journey. I have such an amazing team of specialists outside of Kaiser.....the smartest nutritionist ever; the help of an advocate doctor who is also spiritual and has helped me tremendously with both information about cancer as well has helping me connect to my heart and spirit; the most compassionate meditation teacher who is helping me overcome decades of self-loathing and realizing self love and forgiveness is possible; dance and sound and music therapy from dear friends to help my heart connect to what is really true; an acupuncturist/ healer who addresses more than the physical world, but helping me with my grief while treating me, helping me heal past traumas; healing circles that help me remember the greater forces of love that carry me all the time.

I also have the most amazing circle of friends and family. You who let me know you are praying for me, loving me, sending positive healing thoughts, reminding me that this body, this journey, is just part of the big picture. Your support is the highlight of my life. It means so much to me to hear from you. Also, thank you to those of you who love cooking and bring us the most delicious meals made with love. It has been so nice to eat that delicious and nurturing food and thank you for taking into consideration my special dietary needs. Thank you for the eggs from your chickens....I'm trying to only eat things that have love in them and I know you love your chickens and give them a good life. I love the cards with inspirational and positive words, the flowers, the poems you send me. I've loved the visits (when I'm up for it), I love the game nights...so good for laughter and would love to have more of you come over to play games or watch movies. I love meeting you for hikes on the beach or even just around my house on days I can't go too far. Walking is good for getting things moving in my body and sometimes the motivation of you coming here to walk with me is gets me out of the house. Thank you to those who have reached out to (and even paid for) certain practitioners that have given me complementary treatments. Thank you for contributing financially to some of the expenses that come with this territory. I feel so blessed! There are really no words to express how this makes me feel. But THANK YOU so much. I couldn't do this journey alone and while this is my karma (and I hope I'm burning a lot of it for me, for my ancestors and for my children), this is my lonely journey, I am accompanied by such a force of love and support. It's really palpable. I only hope you can feel the love and gratitude I have for you because it is BIG in my heart. I hope you feel it reflecting back to you, filling you in the same way your love fills me.

I also have the best family in the world. I imagine some families fall apart during times of extreme stress, during times when one has a disease that brings the reality of death in close proximity. It is hard sometimes for me to know how this affects my children. Having cancer is not just a solitary experience because it affects the family with a whole gamut of emotions. My family are my champions. Steve is by my side 100%. He accompanies me to all my doctor appointments (and there are plenty...almost twice a week). He fills out forms, does research when I'm too burned out to or don't want to read about another poor prognosis for the kind of cancer I have, he wakes me to give me my medicine if needed. He takes me to the ER and sits for hours. He is an angel and I'm so fortunate to have this angel by my side. I know he'd hate me saying this, but if any of you cook vegetarian meals for yourself and feel you'd like to include an extra person in that meal, I bet he'd love to partake. I make a lot of broths and things that really aren't fulfilling and I'm sad he is eating burritos (though he loves them) and/or frozen meals. I wish I could whip up something better than steamed veggies/millet/tofu...so if it's EASY for you to cut a piece of your yummy meal and bring it over, I know he'd love it (sorry Steve....just had to mention this).

My son Nathan flew all the way from Bali for my surgery, then flew back, got his family and came back to Santa Cruz for 2.5 months. He helps me realize I'm stronger than I think. He is my champion of strength. My house was filled with so much love and activity when they were here. My grandchildren writing me notes telling me I'm strong and loved, everyone being so supportive. How did I get so lucky? Then my Kusum...my first born, my nurse (at times). Always looking out for me...wanting me to implement better self care. She monitors who can come over, has implemented hand sanitizer for guests because it's flu season and my WBC [white blood count] is low right now. She wants to fill my heart with positive energy, sharing meditations, blankets with positive words on them, Team Leslye shirts. She gives me injections twice a week (my grandson held my hand when he was here...giving me good support and seeing shots aren't as scary as he believed). We cry together (we're both quite expressive with ALL our emotions), we walk, and we share this journey in an intimate way. My son Corey....who always wants to make sure all my needs are met. He will cook for me, prepare things I can eat, will make sure I stay on schedule with my supplements. He is a natural caretaker. He has such a gentle and intuitive side to him...which makes for a great caretaker. He is on call if I need anything. He will accompany me to any appointment Steve can't, even though those are very rare. He makes sure I'm warm enough or comfortable at all times. He'll walk with me, not bothered by my slow pace at times.

Steve's children have been there for me too. I feel their love and support and offers to make things like bone broth. I feel bad because Steve has work and his own needs to take care of and then he's on full time with me. I don't want the family to feel neglected at all...and I miss seeing them, especially my (step) daughter Tara and her boys because they live in Cotati and work or do sports all the time. I thank them for their understanding that this is hard for us and we miss them terribly. I hope we can see them more often as I adjust to getting my treatments and don't need so many doctor appointments.

I know this is a long and rambling letter....I just wanted to let you all know how important you are to me, how much your support means to me, how I feel your love and it fills me and accompanies me wherever I go. I am humbled and honored by the immense love and support. I hope you know that it also reflects back to you, that we are enveloped in this circle of love and grace.

Thank you for being part of my life.
xoxoxoxox
Leslye/Mukti

March 1, 2020

Hello All,

It's been awhile since I've written. I think a combination of being depressed and tired and busy with appointments....but I'd like to try to give a little update. Forgive me if I'm repeating information. I have to say my brain is not the sharpest these days :-)

Before I get into things, I want to acknowledge the gratitude I feel for each and every one of you. Because of you, I am moving forward. You have created a sacred space for me in your thoughts, your words, your actions. Wherever this uncertain journey will lead, one thing is for sure....I am surrounded and filled with love. I try to remember that as I walk through these unknown roads, with unknown destinations. However, having this amazing circle of support offers a healing for my heart and soul I never imagined. So, thank you for being part of this with me!

This journey can surprise me with emotions I'd rather not feel. I never knew what real depression was. Now, it hits hard sometimes. And nothing I do, whether it's listen to a dharma talk, mediate, sing, or cry, will lift the cloud. I'm coming to accept it is part of the experience. I wish I could say I'm happy and positive all the time. Things happen and out of the blue, bam, hello depression. I think sometimes it comes because I wonder if I'm doing the right thing. Should I increase the one drug I'm doing low dose? Should I stop taking so many supplements? Who do I trust? There are so many contradicting voices. When I start doubting things, my head spins and I feel lost. Thank goodness there are some times when I can connect to my inner self and find guidance and trust. For example, after a meditation the other day, I asked myself, should I continue with chemotherapy? Chemotherapy is intense. It destroys good cells, creates painful side effects, feels like it makes my body weaker. So I question if it's right for me. I get quiet and listen. The voice says yes, keep going. Keep going right now. I'm being treated by an amazing team of nutritionists, herbalists, therapists, acupuncturists, body workers, holistic doctors, etc. Trust. Trust. Trust this right now. When I lose the ability to trust, I ask Steve. Steve comes to almost every appointment with me, asks questions, feels deep into the situation, listens, takes notes and records the conversations. So, when I lose my ability to trust because I'm lost in depression, he is my compass. He is my guide.

I find I don't think about death as much as Idid when I was first diagnosed. I used to feel so removed from life around me, thinking I wasn't here for much longer and wanted to live in to that. I would observe people doing their lives...buying stamps at the post office, having coffee and pastries at the bakery, buying fresh organic veggies at the farmers market while meeting people and listening to the music and enjoying the sunshine. I saw all this going on without me. I know it sounds morbid, but that was just where my mind went. Now I look at this differently. I walk the line of fighting for my health, of doing what I can to prevent a recurrence, while at the same time, I see and acknowledge the reality of having cancer. I am living life and accepting the love offered. I know the proximity of death is closer to me than I believed it was before knowing I had cancer. I am scared of what death looks and feels like yet I feel I must make peace with this. I'm still learning what this means.

The will to live is not the denial of death, but the intensification of a life experience, which comes with the realization of how finite life truly is.
(I can't remember where I read this quote or who to attribute it to)

However, I'm feeling great, feeling strong (most of the time), and feeling healthy. My herbalist said he's going to make me a superwoman, so I'm going to rise to the role!

This month I'll have an MRI to look at that lymph node in my neck. It feels scary to explore this. I had swelling in my groin (still do) and my first thought was it's cancer. Luckily it doesn't seem likely. It's not a hernia, which was the second thought. It's likely swollen lymph nodes according to the ultrasound. And maybe edema there as well. I wonder if it's lymphedema, as some people tend to get that. When these little things pop up (like the swelling in my ankles, the swelling in my groin, the pain in my belly), it creates fear for me. I'm working on this. I have been a fearful person my whole life and one would think facing what I'm facing now, I'd overcome that tendency. However, habits are hard to break. Filled with so much love, I still fall back in fear. I'm working on it...really, I am :-) I'll have a CT scan the end of the month to make sure the stomach pains are just a side effect of the chemotherapy and not an adhesion or anything worse. Since I don't have a tumor, it's hard to know if the chemotherapy is doing anything for me. But I suppose getting scanned to make sure there are no growths is a good way to measure sometimes.

I've been enjoying the weather now that it's warmer. I love getting out in the fresh air and moving my legs. I love the smell of the air when I'm surrounded by trees, or the ocean as long as I avoid the seal poop/pee smell. I'm part of a 12 week study on colon cancer and exercise during chemotherapy treatment. It's pretty cool because they sent me a Fitbit (to keep) which tracks my steps and my sleep. They want to study survival rates and how exercise might play a part in this. I see it as part of the whole picture of healing.

I apologize for my lack of responses. Sometimes I just don't have it in me to talk. My friend had a code she would send to people....sending three hearts to acknowledge receipt of the communication but not able to respond at the time. I love hearing from you, and your words of encouragement mean a lot to me...Thank you!!!

Much much love to all of you, my amazing circle of support and love. Thank you!
Big hugs,
Leslye

March 22, 2020

What strange times right now! As if cancer wasn't enough to deal with! The four of us in my house have been isolating. Santa Cruz has a shelter in place anyway last week. But I've requested all who live here to not go into stores or anything. So we have people shopping for us and leaving on porch. We walk outside but avoid being near anyone who might be passing. My daughter was sick with a cold so she hasn't been to my house in weeks. We've started meeting for walks (keeping 6 ft distance) It sucks because she took a leave of absence to be with me. I've had a dry cough and tightness in the chest so we're being extra cautious. It's a little scary to know my white blood cells are low so I'm more vulnerable. But I'm imagining my body to be strong anyway!

Last week was chemotherapy #5. I was a little reluctant to go with everything so crazy around us. I think I'll have to evaluate each two weeks whether I'll do it, as each treatment takes its toll on my body...and I believe it's a cumulative effect. I am having a low dose with one drug that would probably be wiping out my system if I got the regular dose. Still, I need to ask myself each time if I should do it.

I am taking a huge herbal protocol with a variety of things that both build my system and attack the cancer cells. I take some cyto toxic herbs. I just have to put my trust in the clinical herbalist I'm seeing.

We've been watching a docuseries called *Radical Remission*. Based on the book with same title. Earlier in my diagnosis I didn't think I had what it takes to believe I was a candidate for this. But I am breaking through and digging to find the belief that I can beat this...and even if my oncologist doesn't think I'm making the right choice by taking low dose chemotherapy, I'm believing what I'm doing is right for me. It's hard not to get sucked into the "evidence based" (that's a loaded statement) standard of care road of the doctor and be a pioneer and advocate for doing this my way. I have to trust it's not solely based on the fear of permanent side effects and know that my body has an intelligence to want to heal and it tells me what's right.

April 1, 2020

<u>Living with cancer in the age of covid19</u>

I suppose the title can be flawed because I'm hoping I'm not living with cancer. I hope the surgery got it all and if there were micrometastatic cells floating around in my body, the chemotherapy I'm doing, as well as the amazing herbal protocol I'm on, is taking care of that.

Perhaps I should say, living with chemotherapy in the time of covid19.

Three weeks ago, we were just being cautious about shaking hands, giving hugs, etc. But we felt safe to stand near each other to take pictures, we hiked and chatted, we visited art museums, we celebrated milestones with events. We shopped fir food, mailed packages at the post office. Gathered for game night. My daughter came to my house, did her homework, played games and watched movies.

In the last two weeks, everyone in my household stopped going to public places. We're talking to our friends and family members out our door while they are at the bottom of the stairs or in their cars. Friends (oh THANK YOU!!!!) are grocery shopping for us. Or running errands. They leave our stuff on the porch. We sanitize it all and then put it in a room for a day or two (unless it needs to be refrigerated). It feels so impersonal to a person like me who loves to connect, to sit with a cup a tea and chat with friends, to gather and play games together, to hike together, catching up. Iso appreciate my family who have sacrificed their social lives (social lives during a shelter in place???) to avoid possible infection. Since people can transmit this virus when they are asymptomatic, one never knows what germs are being passed on. I'm in a category that is more high risk...I'm 60 and I have an immune system that is not quite wonder woman. I'm trying...but not quite there yet! So I had to set up my home life and rules to feel as safe as possible. Thank you Steve, Corey and Leighan for being locked up with me.

We've been able to occupy ourselves with games, chats, movies and books. I still have days when I can't get everything on my list accomplished. I've been getting out for walks as much as possible (the rainy days are a little challenging), avoiding the occasional person or two I see walking. We've been watching a docuseries called *Radical Remission*, stories of people who beat the odds. I'm trying to be one of those. When I was first diagnosed, I picked up the book and as I read through it, I didn't feel my spirit was up to the challenge. Cancer was a death sentence. Chemotherapy was a death sentence. I couldn't shake that thought. I struggle from time to time with that because I have lost so many family members and friends to this disease.

Since I began this letter, my mental health has declined. My nervous system is infected. Infected with fear, unease, stress. Dealing with cancer was difficult enough. I had to dig deep to find strength and trust. I got depressed from time to time and I've had to surrender to something I never thought I'd be living through. The fear of chemotherapy, the fear of cancer growing in other places in my body, the fear of dying. Suddenly, I feel the pain of that diagnosis again. It is bigger and more scary because the risk of catching this virus feels like living in the jungle, where you never know where danger is lurking. The tiger, the snake could be waiting to pounce at any minute. The stress of that is too much. I feel I'm walking on a tightrope, high above the scary, craggy bottom. One end of the rope has cancer sawing away at it, the other end of the rope has covid19 sawing away. I feel trapped. Even when I walk outside, I feel danger is lurking...did the person who walked this road before me cough and leave virus droplets on the street? In the air? Are they imbedding in my clothes? Getting into my nostrils? It is irrational for certain, yet I can't shake the feeling of danger wherever I go.

Getting my blood drawn, I got to the lab when they opened. The lab is in the same building as urgent care. I wanted to be the first person in the lab. Luckily I was, although a woman came down the stairs from urgent care and went to the pharmacy, just a across the hall from the lab. She was masked up and I stayed at least 15 feet behind her as I walked to the lab, I had a cloth mask and a surgical mask on, gloves, glasses and two layers of clothing. I disinfected the chair I sat in and asked Christine (the tech...getting to know these brave people who draw my blood every two weeks) to please wear a mask. I was pleased she put on new gloves after entering my info on the computer. As soon as I was finished, I discarded my gloves at the exit door, peeled off the outer layer of clothing, stuffed it in a bag, put my glasses and ID card in a plastic bag, had Steve squirt hand sanitizer on my hands, and got in the car to go home. I stripped my clothes off at the back door and went directly into the hot shower where I scrubbed from head to foot, while tears flowed from my eyes.

I've cried so much this past week I thought I'd exhaust my tears. But they're endless. I must possess the Pacific Ocean in my body. Sometimes I wonder if they could carry the virus as they flow down my face and sometimes into my mouth. See, I'm neurotic.

Life is completely and utterly different in an instant. I feel the fear for my son, who has a family to support but no income right now. His work depends on travel, which is not happening. I miss my daughter being with me in my house. My fear of the outside world infecting my safe space has cut off allowing anyone inside. I go for walks outside with her and we keep a big distance. CDC says 6 ft. I prefer 10 with her and 100 or more if anyone is walking by. I know so many in this world are now suffering....the loss of work, perhaps relatives getting sick...it saddens me.

I don't want to die right now. Not with the world like it is. I think about this sometimes.

I know this is not an uplifting letter and you might wish for me to seek help (I have), or calm my thoughts (I try), or be more positive for my own well being. I find moments where I can relax and I treasure them. I wanted quality of life while I go through cancer treatment. That has an entirely new meaning. I grab those minutes of respite. I sometimes rely on Valium (it was 3:30 am when I resumed writing this letter...I'm holding off on the Valium until later today) to get me through a day. I hum, I meditate, I participate in zoom meetings for support. We attended the Unitarian Universalist service via zoom last Sunday and then participated in small group conversation. I'm going to create a network of support to reach out to when I get panicked. Let me know if you're willing to accept my calls when I'm spinning into despair. Or if you want to do a sound healing, a singing healing, a dancing healing, a writing group, a virtual book club (if we have the same books), etc. I feel the need for some sense of normality.

At 11:00 today, I head to the infusion center for my 6th chemotherapy treatment. That's halfway to 12! I am taking it treatment by treatment as I weigh the risk vs benefit of treatment. So far, my blood work as been holding up. My neutrophils are low, as usual for chemotherapy. But my liver enzymes have improved. My blood counts are good. My body is strong despite my nervous system falling apart. I'm going to focus on the strength of my body, the intelligence of the cells to want to do everything possible to be healthy and robust. I'm going to focus on how held I am by your love, prayers and support. I'm bringing that with me to my treatment, a shield of protection. Love is stronger than fear. I already feel better just saying that.

I can't thank you enough for all the love and support you give me. Thank you for allowing me to express my fears on this journey. Thank you for helping me find strength to go forward. It is a huge part of healing. I know, wherever I am, I am held in love. I appreciate the care and connections. You all are part of my healing journey. My heart is full. Thank you! I love you.

May we all have ease and peace,
Leslye/Mukti

April 13, 2020

Dancing with Fear
(warning: very candid stream of consciousness)

"Breathing in, I hold my fear with tenderness. Breathing out, I care for my dear little fear."
Thich Nhat Hanh

Fear. I am feeling a lot of fear lately. The fact is, I have lived with fear for most of my life. Maybe as a teenager I was fearless. I took risks I would never take today. I was reckless. Driven by an unrealized need to feel loved, I found myself in plenty of perilous situations. Drugs numbed the insatiable black hole for me. Luckily, at 16 years old, a power bigger than me intervened. A series of events led me to a yoga temple. It happened that the yoga teacher was a counselor at a camp I'd gone to when I was younger. They offered yoga classes taught to them by their teacher, Baba Hari Dass. As fate would have it, that was the teacher I'd wanted to meet after a friend brought back a brochure from the Lama Foundation, where she'd gone to do a retreat with Ram Dass. Had I not spent two sleepless nights high on speed, smoking pot to calm myself down, relentlessly talking to myself, I would not have realized the trajectory of my life was heading towards that which I was all too familiar with....drug addiction. Like I said, by some amazing grace, I took a sharp turn. Still living a fearless life, I found a ride to California the summer I turned 17 (I put up a sign in a juice bar looking for a ride). Someone was watching over me....the man dropped me off in Santa Cruz. It would have been a challenge to know where to go...I didn't even have a map (I think fearless should be read as stupid) and I'd never been to California.

My only possessions were whatever fit in the backpack I took with me. And here in Santa Cruz I landed. I didn't recognize my fear, but it certainly ruled my life. I didn't know it then, but I had a big fear of people. No drugs, no wild life, no drinking to cover up my insecurities. Instead, a lot of people with strong foundations, a lot of education and a deep connection to others who studied with Baba Hari Dass. I was intimidated and never felt good enough. My fear prevented me from developing deep relationships. These people had strong egos, were mostly older than me, and seemed to have it all together. I didn't recognize my fear, but it controlled my actions...or lack of actions.

My fear became magnified when I had children. I was 19 when my first child was born....and the feeling of invincibility was replaced by vulnerability. Being vulnerable meant being weak. I tried to stuff it down, but fear prevailed. I suddenly became afraid of flying. I worried about everything. Being attached to a child brought out the fear of death big time. I was no stranger to death. My father died when I was 9 years old. The man my mother was in a relationship with after that, whom I loved so much, was murdered when I was 11 years old.

Life went on, and fear dominated. I didn't allow myself to trust the love that was in my life. I never felt I deserved it, or that anyone would really love me. Fear controlled my life. I always imagined the worst case scenario. Geez.....it's like confession time here! You're getting a glimpse of a history I'm not proud of. Let's just say, I lived in fear...every fear you can imagine...fear of new places, fear of meeting new people, fear of getting hurt, fear of not being liked, fear, fear, FEAR! I didn't know Thich Nhat Hanh's words....I didn't know how to hold fear in tenderness, to care for my fear....didn't know how to hold myself in tenderness.

Cancer has made me confront my fear in the ways I never knew possible. I lived many years with fear of medicines, or, really, side effects. I've lived with fear of medical instruments in my body. That is one reason I never had a full colonoscopy. I feared the scope would puncture my intestine and I'd be sicker than I felt most of my life living with IBS. Damn fear!

Fear of surgery! That is a huge one! The thought of being cut open makes my heart beat with anxiety. Yet, when you have a tumor that is blocking the intestine, surgery is necessary, no options at all.

Fear of dying. That's a huge one. I haven't yet mastered that one. I try. While I want to live, having cancer brings the proximity of death an arms length away. I can touch that door. I try to hide from it but I know it's right there. Granted, this is the fate for all of us....can't have life without death. Yet there is something about being here, in this body, in this life, with this family, with these friends, in this house, hiking on this breathtaking trail, breathing the earthy air, watching this amazing sunset, feeling the sand in between these toes, laughing from this throat, hugging with these arms, dancing with these feet, smiling with this mouth, crying from these eyes....it makes confronting a hard thing to do. Yet it is necessary. It doesn't mean my will to live through this is gone....it just means the reality of my end might be closer than I was ready for. So it means getting ready for it sooner. And what does that mean? I'm finding it means living each moment in that moment...feeling the feelings that arise. Crying the tears that need to be cried. Laughing and singing and appreciating the beauty that is here. Feeling the love that is here. Giving love...letting my beautiful family and friends know how much love I have for them. Feeling for life beyond this body. Knowing that the infinite that exists outside of me also exists inside of me....

But I have no idea what death is like. I can only imagine. Actually, I can't imagine. Morbid as it might sound, I've sometimes thought about life after I die. I've imagined myself in a casket, people surrounding the body. I imagine, yet it's really scary, this body being put into the fire, to be reduced to a container of ashes. I do this to try to make peace with it. But I haven't found freedom from the fear of death.

Fear of chemotherapy. I associated chemotherapy with death. Cancer and chemotherapy meant death. It was a lose/lose situation. That is why I got immensely depressed after my surgery. Having 14 lymph nodes positive for cancer meant chemotherapy. Having 14 lymph nodes positive for cancer meant death. There was no way out...until I found out I could have SOME chemotherapy...like a small dose of chemotherapy. Or at least of one of the various chemotherapy agents they administer. So, I chose the cowardly path of only getting a tiny dose of the agent that causes the worst side effects. Who wants to have their nerves worked on? Who wants to feel like they're swallowing pebbles or glass for days? Who wants to get electric shocks for days when opening the mouth to eat? Who wants neuropathy in the hands and feet...sometimes (often) becoming a permanent affliction? Well, after 6 treatments of low dose, I discovered who might want to deal with side effects....those who want a fighting chance to outsmart the cancer cells. Earlier this week, I had a second opinion and was reminded that I have an aggressive form of colon cancer. The pathologist laid out the report in a way that struck fear inside me once again. "Very aggressive cancer" "Invaded vascular system and nerves" "Large tumor that grew through the intestine" "14 lymph nodes positive" and on and on and on. It was a reminder I didn't need to hear. Or maybe I did. Because it gave me the push to up the dose of that oxaliplatin. I'm going from 30% to 45% this week. And if all goes well, I'll up it again. I will stop at 60% because 6-8 treatments of 60% increases the odds of overall survival.

I don't want this aggressive beast to show up in my body (hoping it hasn't already...haven't had a CT scan to check) again! I don't want more surgery. I don't want to have more chemotherapy when I'm done with this. So, I'll up the dose. I'll be brave, I'll deal with the side effects. I won't do it without complaints though....sorry to say. I hate the side effects now. But I'm so fortunate. I have the guidance of an herbalist who is helping my body be strong...I'm on a robust protocol so I can be robust and resilient. Drugs were never my friend, and now I embrace them. I also go into this battle with the force of Love with me. If I can focus on the love, then even when i'm walking the path to the other world, I'll be fulfilled. I'm going to drink deep all the love and prayers.

We are living in strange times. Strange and scary times. I won't go into the politics or talk about the scary monster who has blood on his hands already. Suffice to say it adds a lot of anxiety and fear to my life. It almost broke me. Yet, there is a resilience there that is helping me bounce back. Yes, I have created a safe space here in my little house. And that is what I'll continue to do...ignore the news and get on with the task of fighting cancer in a time of restricted living.

I apologize if I don't respond to the emails in a timely manner. It means the world to me to have your support and love and prayers. If I don't write back, it is only because I've gotten lost in my own world.....not because I don't want to. I will try harder, even if only to say thank you.

This Wednesday will be treatment #7. I've crossed the halfway point. It will be with an increased dose of the scary drug....hey, i'm being filled with platinum.....between that and the gold crowns I have on my teeth, this body is going to be worth something :-)!!!! I could use those prayers to help me through this....hoping the side effects will be manageable, short lived, and my body will be strong and continue to defeat any rogue cancer cells that might be floating around in there. My body is not wanting to be a host to them anymore.

I will close with a little saying from my beloved midwife who lived an amazing life filled with so much love, and passed with the abundance of love filling and surrounding her (Thank you Bob for sending me this)

I have learned that bravery comes,
not from fearlessness,
but from a real intimacy with fear.
~Roxanne Potter

Love and peace
Leslye/Mukti

May 1, 2020

I was writing an email about my wonderful caregivers. However, since it was at 3 am, i'm not finished yet.
I wanted to share the news from my CT scan yesterday.
I'd been having really bad cramping for 2 weeks and we postponed my chemotherapy on Wednesday. I had a CT scan on Thursday.
Talk about anxiety...waiting for the results. Wanting to know, but not wanting to know. I'd seen some

bad news of people with this aggressive signet ring cancer recently and got sad.

I needed to know if tumors were causing my pain. Or if something was wrong with my surgical sites. The report came back and said NO RECURRENT MASS or METASTATIC DISEASE IDENTIFIED!

So, right now, it looks like I have no cancer growing inside. My liver even looks good. 5 more chemotherapy treatments and I'm done! I'll be having another radiologist reading this and comparing to my past results. But right now, we're crying tears of joy! And I wanted to share this with you...my amazing support system. I would not be feeling as good as I do without all the love, support, and prayers you send my way.

Thank you all so much!!!!
Leslye/Mukti

June 3, 2020

Hello All

As I look at receiving treatment for chemotherapy #10, I find it hard to want to write an update about myself.

A cultural uprising has occurred and it's huge! It is a weird time in my personal life to be witnessing this. I'm there 100% with this movement and uprising! Learning about racism and my own personal bias has been a big part of my life. It is what inspired me to open a children's bookstore way back when. But it is not enough! I stand with the Black community in demanding a change to this systemic racism that has existed for centuries. Given my physical health situation right now, I must search for different ways to contribute. Letters, boycotts, phone calls, personal introspection....whatever I can do...I am listening to the people fighting for change.

This uprising is having such a tremendous impact on the world. Not even the mass school shootings, and the resulting marches and actions for change those inspired, impacted the world like this. This energy and power is unstoppable. Could this be the tearing down of systemic racism? I don't have answers...I'm listening.

So, I go to treatment #10 with a heavy heart. I am and always have been a sensitive person. The suffering of others often affects me. I think I don't have a strong constitution. It is easily shaken. It's weird, because I can be a harsh person...and then I always feel bad for being that way. I hate complaining to my doctors about all my side effects, my concerns, my fears. I'm also physically sensitive...and have a low threshold for pain. I'm learning to take the punches though. I do think I'm getting stronger in many ways.

I am going to take a break after my treatment tomorrow. I'm going to extend the start of #11 an extra week. That way, when I begin to feel better on Thur or Fri, I won't have to start getting anxiety and then fasting for chemotherapy the following Wednesday. I'll actually be able to enjoy feeling good for an entire week! Then I'll only have two more treatments left!

I have to admit I'm already scared of a recurrence. I'm in a group online and some of the folks who started just a little before me are getting bad news. There are others who get good news too. Luck of the draw? There is no proven rhyme or reason to this mystery. One can be very educated about their cancer, ask the right questions, seek the best treatments, and not be able to stop the growth.

I realize it's not a matter of being an informed patient. But getting healed is here for all of us.

Healed is a huge word. It is beyond cured. I think being healed must be finding peace.

I'll be getting a liquid biopsy to test for circulating tumor DNA in the blood. It is a tumor informed test. We had to work hard to get this as none of my doctors were interested in this. They say they wouldn't know what to do if the test came back positive. Granted, it is new on the market. But the recent study that came out shows that it's very reliable. The thing is...it can show positive up to 8 months before it's seen on a scan. To me, this is great news because my tumor was a mucinous one...poorly differentiated...and these types are not easily picked up on scans. Some people get laparoscopic surgery as a means of looking for recurrence. Of course, we hope the news will be good...that there is no ctDNA in the blood. I will be tested every 3 months. I'll still need a CT scan and a PET scan (i'll be radioactive after that one) but this may eventually be the tool for less invasive screening measures. I hope so.

I know one thing for sure....I am held by your love and support. I miss you all so much! I want to see you. I want to play games with you. I want to hike with you. I want to sing and dance with you. I want to cook for you. I think life is surreal for most of us (or it's just me projecting). I hope you all are safe, happy, feeling love, getting support and enjoying the trees and birds and flowers. I thank you for all the love and support you send my way. I thank you for the prayers. I thank you for the texts, the calls, the emails. I may be super slow to respond, but I appreciate each one.

Please send those healing thoughts as I receive the 10th chemotherapy treatment.

Thank you, thank you, thank you!

I truly love you

leslye/Mukti

May 28, 2020

I sort of did everything with brakes on and am needing to find a place of self forgiveness.

I've had IBS all my adult life. Had barium enemas, sigmoidoscopy and tried all sort of dietary changes. I realized at some point it could have been caused by childhood trauma. The thing I never got was a colonoscopy because I was SURE my colon would get perforated due to the inflammation that must have existed in there. I also thought it would never be cancer because I had the same pain since I was 17.
So I'm 60 and hadn't had one.

Last year I began getting upper abdominal pain. I finally went to the doctor to rule out pancreatic cancer (I had 3 friends die in the last 2 years of that). She wanted to rule out an ulcer. So after many tests for that, and all negative, didn't know what else to do.

I went to Bali in the summer (one of my sons live there with his family) thinking I could be sick there as well as here. We usually just hang out at home and the beach. I was dealing with extreme fatigue for months but thought I could handle it. I just felt worse and worse and finally had a CT scan in Malaysia. They saw a mass and the radiologist said it could be Crohn's. The GI doc said it was probably intestinal bacteria and gave me antibiotics. I stopped pooping eventually and stopped eating because it hurt.

Came back to California in September, had a colonoscopy and bam...cancer

I had to get an endoscopy because it was signet ring and they wanted to rule out stomach as a primary cancer source. It was a long procedure because I wanted to be put to sleep.

I was scared of surgery and put it off until October 23.

I was scared of chemotherapy (my mom died from leukemia and I saw how chemo affected her) so I didn't start it until 3 months after surgery.

I have not had a full dose of oxaliplatin. I started with 25% and am up to 45%.
I get full dose of 5-FU.

So I didn't get aggressive with chemicals. But I'm being as aggressive as I can. I'm also working with an integrative practitioner.

I hate myself for rejecting a colonoscopy way back in my 30's and 40's. More because I don't want my children to suffer. I won't see how hard it is for them to watch me go through this. I love them so much and hate myself for being careless. But this is my thing to get over.
I hope after treatment I won't see a recurrence. I have 3 more to go. I'm going to have a liquid biopsy to see about early detection.

I am older and hope that doesn't lessen my chances of recovery. However I am learning the difference between healed and cured. I am going for both. I want healing for everyone, whatever my outcome is.

July 7, 2020

Tomorrow begins the 12th of 12 chemotherapy treatments. After that, no more ice packs filling our freezer, no more containers of little ice cubes made by my love so he can spoon feed me for 2.5 hours during the oxaliplatin infusion. No more fasting for 3.5 days every other week (BTW, I'm gaining weight despite that!!! Today, 98 pounds...the highest since my diagnosis). This will be the last shot of lidocaine in my chest so the 1 inch needle can be inserted into my port...the port that has a catheter attached to it and enters a vein in my neck which reaches down to my heart. No more going home on Wednesday with a pump full of chemotherapy attached to the port, rhythmically administering the drug with a little "whrrr" every other minute until it is empty sometime on Friday.

My oncologist fired me after my treatment #11. I think my getting a liquid biopsy was the last straw for her. She is very compassionate, caring and conservative. Because I belong to an amazing colon cancer support group that has people from all over the world who have been through or are going through this, as well as oncologists who comment on clinical trials or sometimes just answer some of the questions we post, I have learned of new and cutting edge tests. Admittedly, even the oncologists say it is like flying the plane while building it. There isn't protocol about what to do if the results are positive. However, it has been through clinical trials and it is very promising in terms of watching for recurrence. It is a tumor informed blood test that checks for circulating tumor DNA. It has false negatives, but is very accurate on the positives. Of course, just as my treating oncologist said, I'll have anxiety and be nervous knowing the results since there is no way they will treat without evidence of a tumor. However, because the typical blood markers are not indicators for me (mine were super low even with the tumor inside), and because I have a rare and aggressive form of colon cancer that is hard to see with CT scans, MRI and PET scans, I feel we have a method of detecting something, which would alert us to the need for scans, or explorative surgery. Because of covid, the world of telemedicine has opened up opportunities to have consultations with oncologists all over. I was fortunate to find a one who has been so caring, is a specialist in colon cancer, is very involved with his patients, and is brilliant. We feel fortunate to be able to work with him. I hope my new treating oncologist will be open to communications with him as well. Otherwise I might have to move to Iowa :-)

The results of my liquid biopsy have been sent to my surgeon but she's been away. We've been nervously awaiting the results. What will I do if it's positive? Will I lose hope? Will it feel the same way it felt when I was originally diagnosed? I am very aware of the poor prognosis this kind of cancer has. I try very hard not to read about it and let that imprint my mind and spirit. I have found quite a few people who have survived...one woman is 12 years NED (no evidence of disease)!! That is amazing!

When I was first diagnosed, I felt the need to come to terms with dying. In fact, I felt very removed from reality. I would do an errand and feel I was sort of a ghost....feeling as if I was already slipping into a different reality...one where life goes on, but without me. Celebrating the holidays with my family, my mind kept telling me this could be the last time I'll be with these beautiful people. Knowing I needed chemotherapy added a feeling of "I'll die if I do and I'll die if I don't." I felt I was put in a box with no exit...only death. As time went on, and I felt strong, I stopped thinking about dying all the time. However, when dealing with pain, the thought of dying pops right up. I never know if it's a result of side effects or if there is cancer causing it. If you've received my prior emails, you will know I've been on an emotional roller coaster. Not only dealing with cancer, but dealing with a global pandemic that has made connection with my loved ones difficult, as I'm sure many of you are experiencing. My family cannot visit from Bali this summer as planned. I want to see them again!!! I have no idea if there is cancer in my body (though I might have a clue once I get the results), I have no idea why cancer takes some people and spares others. I both live with hope and the knowledge that I have to learn to face death.

A silver lining of this pandemic has been the access to my community online. I can participate in classes with the cancer support center which adds a comforting routine to my life. I can join my spiritual family with classes three days a week and I've enjoyed that sense of normalcy and connection. I can sing with a circle of uplifting, life affirming friends. There have been many ways to connect. While I watch a lot of people jumping back into life, and knowing I just can't do that yet, this has been a blessing.

As you can probably tell, I'm all over the place with this writing...stream of consciousness to the extreme. With "chemo brain" and extremely high pitched ringing in my ears, it's choppy. Top it off with letting my fingers do the walking and no rereads or edits, I can only apologize for any lack of flow.

I cannot express the gratitude I have for so much love in my life. Thank you for everything...for being present on the weird zoom calls, for calling when you go shopping to see if we need anything, for sending good wishes, prayers and love. I love getting your letters/emails and hearing how things are going in your life. I hope everyone is healthy and safe! These are trying times in so many ways. I send my love and good wishes to all of you. I'll end with the beautiful loving kindness meditation as given by Anam Thubten:

May you be safe from inner and outer harm.
May you be free from guilt, shame and hatred.
May you enjoy physical and mental well being.
May you live with the ease of an open heart.
May you be wakened to your true nature, which is an inexhaustible source of love, compassion and wisdom.

Blessings and Peace,
Leslye/Mukti

July 7, 2020

I was sitting at the infusion center getting the anti-nausea meds and IV fluids and getting my chemo pump disconnected, with tears in my eyes.
The oncologist who has treated me since January has given up on me and passed me to her partner, unbeknownst to me. So when I got there, Dr Yen came in to talk with me. He is very energetic (I've seen him in action every Friday I'm there), makes himself available to all his patients, somewhat arrogant, and seems middle of the road. He told me he's taking over and we talked. I think doctors

don't like when patients do research, sit in on webinars with other oncologists, ask questions about care that is out of the box, etc. But I told him that is just how I am.

He wants me to get my port taken out after I'm finished. The other doctor told me to keep it in for a year. Others keep it for 2 years. I don't like the port and it does create problems, including blood clots. So I understood where he was coming from. But I asked him what if I have a recurrence? He said it would be a disaster if I did, and getting a new port would be the last of my problems....that basically I'm going to die if I have a recurrence. I told him I have met many people who have stage 4 colon cancer and are alive years....getting treatments on and off as the tumor grows or stabilizes. He said, "Do they have signet ring cells?" and I couldn't answer him. So basically, I'm being told they will adhere to regular colon cancer surveillance guidelines even though I have an aggressive cancer that will "most likely kill me if it comes back" instead of stepping outside the box and searching for ways to find this at its earliest stages. So, what I'm hearing is, yes, you have an aggressive cancer and no, we're not going to look at any other options than what the cancer institute gives as guidelines for regular colon cancer.

I'm grieving right now....I have to not let my spirit get sunk. And, I'll have to look for insurance that allows me to find an oncologist/specialist and work with them. I already told Steve if I have to drive to Iowa or Ohio, I will. But I'll need the insurance to cover the medical costs.

The few things he said that I liked is he is open to talking to an oncologist I already consulted with. He even said he sometimes learns things from other doctors (well, well, well!!). And he would have ordered sequencing of my tumor to see what the genetics and genomics of it are....something I fought for because they only do that for stage 4 cancer....but mine being aggressive and stage 3C, I felt it should have been done.

Maybe I'll like him, but I'm not going to let him write me off if I have a recurrence. I think I'll have to talk to him and see if he's willing to do anything possible (within reason, as I have my limits too) to help me if I have a recurrence.

July 8, 2020

You may or may not have detected a forced positive attitude about this treatment being my last. Honestly, I thought it was just going to be a break because I was uncertain of what the liquid biopsy would tell. The oncologist said if the test was positive, it would be ominous. However, yesterday he went over next steps just to prepare in case we got bad news...which I appreciate because no one wants to hear something out of left field and not have an idea of what to do next.

This morning before I went to the infusion center, my surgeon told me she had the report but wasn't sure how to interpret in as it is something she has never seen (she has been an advocate for me and signed the release of my tumor tissue so the test could be performed...none of the 3 oncologists I asked would do it). So, in my mind, I thought...if she is having trouble understanding what it says, then it obviously must not be a negative result. I was disheartened, but not 100% surprised as all the pain (which can be due to side effects) I experience makes me think it's cancer.

I emailed my consulting oncologist and let him know what she said. While I was at the infusion center, I checked my email. There was a note from his nurse that said:

"Hi Leslye-

We did get the fax this morning and the report says negative. So YAY for you, that's fantastic. I hope your last chemo goes well!!"

Now I can say.....HOORAY!!!!! 100's of pounds have been lifted off my soul. While I understand that there can be false negatives because I'm actively on chemotherapy, it sure beats having an ominous positive! I'll be retested in a week or two and then again in a few months. I'll be monitored for 2 years like this, as well as CT scans. MRI's and possibly a PET (only if it comes back positive).

NOW I can party!!!!!! Distance party....8 feet apart and masks. When I recover from the side effects that will begin to hit on Friday and last until Wednesday, I'll be free to go! I want to go camping. I want to kayak. I want to experience enjoying nature again. The pandemic or cancer can't take that away!!!

So while I'm cautiously optimistic, I'm rejoicing! And I'm rejoicing because YOU all have helped make this a reality for me. I'm so humbled by all the love and I hope you can feel my love for you. I have learned what it is like to show up for someone. I have learned so much about how to talk to and support people because of the example you've given me. My Steve has been the most giving person I know....everything he does to help me and support me as well as being the shoulder that receives the gallons of tears that pour from my eyes. I feel blessed and I send all these blessings out to all of you!!!!!!!!

Jai Gurudev! Jai Hanuman!

Biggest hugs to all of you

Leslye/Mukti

October 7, 2020

I have had so many good tests (colonoscopy, liquid biopsy, blood work), yet I have suddenly developed a lot of pain. It is similar to, but not exactly the same, as what I felt before I found out I had cancer. I am suspecting there might be a blockage forming from scar tissue. It is constant yet ranges in intensity. I had an appointment with my herbalist today and he will be formulating a powder that has herbs in it that help with scar tissue (gotu kola is one of them, and it reminded me of mornings at your sweet home in Bali). I will also be getting a CT scan and MRI as scar tissue in the bowel is no thing to ignore...often requires surgery to remove it...which can cause more scar tissue, oy vey.

I'd been scared that it is cancer that has come back as this cancer comes into the peritoneum. I've been in touch with too many spouses of people who passed away within months after their recurrence, as they urge me to get laparoscopic surgery to check for cancer. They say their spouses had clear CT scans, and felt good until they didn't, and then it was a matter of months before they passed. I believe my blood work is still very good (thanks to the robust herbal protocol I'm on) that I'd be able to get treatment if they discovered cancer again. I'm gonna fight. And I have an amazing team. I will need to address this pain as it's becoming unbearable at times (but I do have oxycodone left over from surgery if it comes down to that). My best case scenario is this is scar tissue and with a diet change, herbs that address scar tissue, and abdominal massage to break up the strictures, I'll avoid surgery AND feel better. I'm not ready to say goodbye yet (even though we live in dire times).

I wanted to send this "essay" from a man who my youngest son used to study with. Corey did a rite of passage with Tim Corcoran. He has an outdoor school near Mt. Shasta and teaches outdoor survival and living with the earth. He studied with Tom Brown (author of *Grandfather,* and many other books).

Words from Tim…

Looking Forward
One night sitting out on my land I was visited by the Earth Keeper. I was sad and in great fear of losing my way. I was in fear for the future of my commitments to share nature through Headwaters Outdoor School.
This year, 2020, has been brutal for our Earth, and all that lives upon her. I've always worked for the greater good, and my school has been my greatest achievement in my life as an Earth Caretaker and as a teacher. This year has forced us all to take a time out.
I miss the students and the deep relationships I have with my apprentices. I miss the sweat lodges, that magic and that deep Earth connection that they bring. I miss our wonderful meals shared together, cooked with love by Julie and her kitchen crew. I miss waking up every morning with such single-minded purpose to share my love of our Earth with my students, and to infect them with the same passion. It's truly an honor and a gift to be a teacher and mentor.

I've been so lucky to do what I do, always surrounded by wonderful students and staff. I am so grateful for this sacred land I am able to live and work on with the abundance of life within it.

That night I was sitting out, I was fearful of the future. I feared the loss of our school and my use as a teacher. I was afraid that I wouldn't find that sweet spot inside of me that moves me to be the best person I can be. I was afraid of losing my creative edge and desire to start our school up again when it is safe to do so.

Tears came and the Earth Keeper appeared in the trees, and animals arrived as my witnesses. They held me while I cried for our school, for our community and for the Earth. The Earth listened to me as I spoke of my fears. I spoke of global warming and the defining moment it's brought to humans. I feel this Earth shattering moment as a vital time to act to rectify our destruction or it will be too late.

I cried for all the species of animals and plants dying right now due to humans. I feel the hurt from the West Coast fires, the Australian fires and the continued burning Amazon, the melting arctic, the dying coral reefs, the global famines, the Covid-19 virus and the world wide suffering.

I've always felt that empathy is a gift, to be able to feel what other beings feel. That night the feelings were too much for me to carry. Help arrived in a Screech owl, which landed on a willow above me and began calling out. I quieted myself to listen. My sadness and fear turned to wonder and appreciation and connection to our Earth. Hope began to grow within me, and inspiration and ideas.

That warrior in me that never gives up awoke again. A fire began to burn in me, it felt so good. My true self began to take over again, ideas and solutions began to stir. As I looked up at the owl my eyes were drawn to the stars and the Pleiades star system, a place that always gives life to the dreamer in me.

The night became beauty and wonder, and my troubles drifted away. The Earth Keeper let me know that now, this time in history, September 2020, is the time of all time. This is the defining moment for humans and our relationship with our Earth going forward. This is the right time. This is the time when the right people will show up and carry all beings into a beautiful future.

Work is needed to navigate the darkness to reach the light. In a way it's the death of old ways that don't work, and finding the path into a future where our Earth and all living beings are honored and allowed to live in a good way for all life. The right people will show up and lead the way. The Earth Caretaking way.

The Earth Keeper said something so simple and so powerful. He said, "Be the shining light of a star in the darkness. Never stop that light from shining. Never. It's who we humans are when we are at our best, coming from love and kindness. Never give up, fight the good fight. The Earth Caretaker way for our Earth."

The owl flew off and the night went quiet. In that moment I knew that there is no higher purpose to living life than caring for our Earth. It's who I am. It's who we are. So, join me in this epic moment in history. Let's let the light of the stars show us the way through all the chaos and darkness and uncertainty.

As we go through this, we emerge into a healthy Earth cared for by humans. A truly wonderful place to be. A place where all life is honored and flourishes. We must commit to caring for the Earth daily, and stay focused, and continue to learn. We must take action. Things may get much darker for a while, but look for that light, no matter how small

*it seems and follow it. It is your guide to get
through these times. It will illuminate your path.
I believe this is our time. It is our time to take on
this task. We are not here by accident at this time.
We are all Earth Caretakers. We will go about
achieving that in different ways, but this is our
primary life purpose, to be of service. It is your
Calling.
I love our Earth. I love our Headwaters community.
Thank you for making my dreams come true. Our
land here is one of those shining stars. I will
continue to care for the land and keep our school
alive and well far into the future. It is my Calling
and I will follow that Call. You have my word.*

December 5. 2020

I got my liquid biopsy results and they don't look
so good.
But I'm changing insurance so I can go to the
better doctors.
We'll come up with a plan next week.
The most likely place I have a recurrence is in the
abdomen. It often doesn't show on scans, but it
grows there. So laparoscopic exploration will give
us answers.
I'm tempted to go to Bali in January before I start
any treatment. Just to see my family once again!!
I feel more prepared this time because I suspected
the pain I'm having could be related to recurrence.
Luckily we're catching it early.
I'll let you know more as we find out.
This is not the news I wanted to share...but I feel I
have a great team this time.

December 6, 2020

Hello my dear friends,

I know you're thinking, yeah, right...she's going to write a short update? Short isn't really in her vocabulary (unless you're talking about my height..short and shrinking).

So much has happened since I sent out an email...I can't even remember when the last one was. Perhaps it was when I finished chemotherapy in July? Who knows, because with cancer and covid, time is really, really non linear (time is non linear in my life anyway, so imagine how compounded this situation makes things).

Finishing cancer treatment (that arbitrary number that is followed with standard of care) leaves one in a very uncertain state of mind. What is next? Is it gone? Will it come back? Is the headache cancer? Is this back pain cancer? What about the constant pressure in my abdomen? Is it post surgical pain? Scar tissue? Cancer? Things that you experience on a regular basis in life suddenly take on a new meaning. At least for this worried mind. Yet, I hear some people now question their coughs, their headaches, or stomach discomforts, wondering if it's covid. So I think for those that experience that, you might understand what it is to have cancer.

Then there are the stories....too sad to repeat here, but shared by well meaning partners, parents, and spouses of people who had this rare form of cancer. But it is also stressed that we are all different. We could have the same cancer, but our bodies are different. We're not statistics. I am not a statistic. I am not a statistic. When I should be chanting OM, OM, OM, my mind is trying to chant and believe I am not a statistic, I am not a statistic.

It's been a little over 4 months since I've finished chemotherapy. It's been 8 months since we've been somewhat isolated from our friends and most of our family. But yesterday, my son in Ball said he wants to come here with the family, quarantine, then spend some time with me...being part of our isolated little bubble. I didn't want him and the rest to come because of covid and the political situation in this country. Such division, so much hatred out there...I don't want them to experience it. But in our little bubble, all is okay. Except...

I got the results of my 4th liquid biopsy. This is the blood test that is going to revolutionize cancer surveillance in the very near future. I happen to have the good fortune to have worked with two oncologists that are cutting edge. Unfortunately, one is in Ohio and one is in Iowa. And they are not on my insurance plan...yet. Anyway, after 3 negative tests, this one came back positive for circulating tumor DNA in my blood. What makes this test so different and revolutionary is the early detection. In the last month I've had a PET, MRI and CT scan. All were clear. My blood tests have been good. My CEA was never a good indicator for cancer as it was 1 at diagnosis. It was 1.7 this month. So this lets us know there is cancer in my body. The tricky thing is finding it at such an early stage. One person had clear scans like me but when they opened up the belly, there was cancer. Ugh!!

The only thing I have been experiencing consistently is pain in my abdomen, bloating, very mild nausea. Other than that, I feel GREAT!! I've gone for long hikes, I have energy (except when I'm depressed), and I can eat. I've gained weight (almost at my pre cancer weight). But this pain in my abdomen kept speaking out. It's not as bad as it was before I found out I had cancer. Then I was in bed more than out of bed for a few months before I knew what was going on. When I picked up the test results, I felt like I was hit in the stomach. I looked again and again...NO, NO, NO, this can't be true. That was Friday... Stunned, tears, disbelief. I reached out to my online support group. I may have mentioned Colontown (yes, colontown, with "neighborhoods like Rectalburg, Jelly Belly, etc), where there are over 5000 people all over the world dealing with colon cancer. Many are doctors. Many have connections with some of the best GI oncologists in the U.S. I emailed my new doctor in Ohio the results. He emailed me almost immediately and said, "I'm sorry to see this..I hope you're doing okay. We will come up with a plan. You will be okay!" We also began getting texts from our other doctor requesting records. Already I feel held in ways I've never felt. We'll come up with a plan. I'm going to be Ok!! Someone is shining the light for us when we're feeling lost in a very dark place. We'll come up with a plan!! Unfortunately, one of the things I'll probably have to do is have exploratory surgery. For this cancer, it goes into the peritoneum, and seems to hide. That is why it doesn't show on scans. I don't want to have surgery right now with Covid so rampant. I'm hoping I can postpone it because at this point I still feel okay.

But the point to this short letter (did I keep it short?) is I'm looking for a place for my family in Bali. A short term rental here in Santa Cruz. So I'm reaching out to as many people as I can. If you know a realtor who deals with short term rentals, please let me know. If you know someone who has a second home here, or who is leaving for their own winter vacation, please let me know. The minimum time needed is 2 weeks, but we'll take it for 6 weeks. There are 4 of them. But if we found a bigger house, Steve and I would go stay there after their quarantine is over and they tested negative. If you know people who have homes, please give them my email address or ask if I can have theirs. Iso want to see my family from Bali...something I have feared I would not be able to do.

Thank you so very much!!! I'll keep you posted as to our next steps.
I miss seeing everyone so much! I hope you're all doing okay.
Please share your story with me...how has your life been? I can't believe it's been so long since we've been together. Let me know how you are.

Sending so much love, love, love.
xoxox
MuktiLeslye

April 12, 2021

I recently read a post on twitter from an oncologist:

"Someone in the medical field asked me recently, 'Why is it so hard for patients to understand/ remember the details of their cancer?'
Well, imagine if overnight you had to understand the nuances of particle physics. And your life depended on it."

I used to have shame about not finishing college. It's not because I lacked a desire for knowledge, but I lacked steadfast attention and commitment. I was interested in Early Childhood Education as a major. Then Athletic Training. Then Sociology. Then Women's Studies. I probably have more college units than your average college graduate for as many times as I attended community college throughout the decades. I scratch the surface but I don't dive in.

I once owned a children's bookstore. We hosted authors, illustrators, and storytellers and I enjoyed taking them out to dinner. Often, conversations arose about where one went to college. Where was my magic cloak of invisibility? I owned a bookstore after all...I must be an educated intellectual. Nothing could be farther from the truth. I didn't grow up in an academic family nor was I encouraged to plan to attend college. We were a nomad family, like fugitives on the run. Consistency and schooling played a backseat to survival. I was probably sent to school just to be out of the way of my very tired parents who were busy trying to make a living. Grades didn't seem to matter, just attendance. My sister was the first in the family to graduate from college in several generations of our family, though I think she was in her late 20's before she even began to attend school.

No, I'm no scholar. Because I'm not employed now, I have the great fortune to attend several study groups/classes about Yoga Sutras and other ancient Hindu Scriptures every week. A lot of the philosophy goes right over my head. It always did. Unless the reading is about something tangible, I am lost. I hear others discuss their ruminations while I sit silently, listening, hoping to grasp some understanding of the teachings. I'm a kinesthetic learner. I have to experience what I'm learning. But even that has limitations for me. Take music for example. I can learn notes, chords, even hear a beat (well, sometimes I hear the beat...I don't think my former marimba bandmates believed I heard that elusive beat often enough). But hello new language that I don't understand.....Modes? Mixolydian scale? Harmonic scale? I'll never make it past music kindergarten. No, I'm no scholar. I'm a technician.

Getting cancer catapulted me back to school. Colontown University! Yup, a school where I could learn all about colon cancer. Mutations, tumor mutation burden, deep deletions, tumor proteins, cancer stem cells, metronomic chemotherapy, integrative oncology, germline mutations, amplifications, clinical trials, and on and on and on. Words I'd never heard of before. Science is not my language. But I had to learn about this disease. My life depended on this...the quality of my life depended on this. But learning about cancer is not an easy course. Every time I opened an article about my type of cancer I ended up in tears. Nothing like reading the statistics of a disease you have to throw one into a deep depression. There is a fine line between learning enough about cancer and reading too much. It's hard not to get hung up on statistics. It's damn hard not to get hung up on statistics. I try to tell myself I'm not a statistic. No one is. Yet, reading about cancer can really mess with your reality.

Colon cancer often metastasizes to the liver and lungs. Other places it can metastasize to are the brain, the ovaries or the peritoneum (lining of the abdomen). This is where the cancer has now shown up for me....the lining of the peritoneum. The dreaded 'perl mets.' I was at high risk for this....having a T4 tumor (one that has grown through the outer layer of the intestine), perineural and vascular invasion, a poorly differentiated tumor, and signet ring cells. Because I was getting the tumor informed liquid biopsy, and the results became positive in December, we were on high alert for a recurrence. This kind of testing is still very new and there is no standard of treatment for people who have a positive test without clinical evidence of cancer...exactly the situation I was in for months...until now.

I was having some concerning symptoms....bloating in my tummy....pants and bra feeling uncomfortable, feeling full after eating small amounts. But, other than that, I've been feeling GREAT!!!! I've been hiking, camping, eating, dancing, cooking, etc. My weight is back to pre diagnosis (and maybe one or two pounds more) and my energy is high. I've had 9 months of no chemotherapy. My son, daughter in law, and grandchildren came to visit for 2 glorious months (and that was my biggest dream come true) which filled my heart completely. Steve and I went camping on Mt. Tam, something I didn't think I'd ever do again. I am vaccinated against Covid and that has opened up my world again...on a deeper level I feel less stress. This has to be good for my immune system! But the bloating sometimes caused considerable pain. I called my oncologist because I was concerned. We moved up the CT scan I was supposed to have in May and I came in last week. While I knew something was brewing, I was also happy to put it out of my mind. Ignorance really can be bliss. Even with a bloating belly, it's amazing how powerful denial can be. I also intuitively knew that the recurrence would be in the peritoneum. This type of cancer is typically hard to find on scans. I knew a laparoscopic look around was what I needed if nothing showed in these scans. I guess between drinking 1.5 bottles of contrast and what they injected in my veins, which I felt traveling throughout my body, heating every little nook and cranny, creating a panic attack (I'll never get used to how that feels), the cancer showed up. It's not in my liver or lungs. It's in the lining of my abdomen and I will find out how extensive it is when I speak with my oncologist.

This week I'll get more information....a plan of action from my oncologist. I have a consultation with the surgeon. This cancer doesn't often respond to systemic chemotherapy, but I do not have certain mutations which may increase my odds of it responding. Most people with perl mets have "The Mother of All Surgeries," CRS/HIPEC surgery. It is a very long and intense surgery. Don't ask me why, but I watched a video about it...graphic details included.

To say I'm heartbroken is an understatement. Scared doesn't even begin to describe how I feel about my future. I know the consequences of letting this sticky cancer proliferate inside my body. I know I have some features which make this cancer aggressive. I know the risks of chemotherapy and surgery. Even with the integrative care I'm getting, I'm not looking at great odds. But, as science writer and evolutionary biologist Stephen Jay Gould says in his fabulous essay, *The Median Isn't the Message*, "Attitude clearly matters in fighting cancer."

I have lived through hell. Cancer, covid, isolation. I have come out of the dark tunnel of total despair and embraced life again. Embraced it because it is what it is. I'm living with cancer. I'm fighting cancer. I may die because of cancer. But today I'm alive. Today I had another day of talking to friends.

Of walking in the woods with my beloved. Of walking on the beach with my daughter. Of participating in a class studying ancient Hindu scriptures. Of talking to my cancer exercise support buddies. Of slowly eating a handful of chocolate chips, helping get rid of the taste of the 1000's of supplements I just took. Of talking to my son and grandchildren in Bali. Of laughing with a friend I've had since jr. high school. I am trying hard to continue embracing life and feeling joy even as I face this scary disease. Attitude matters and I have to turn on the search lights, learn as much as I can so I can make informed decisions. Attitude matters and I must engage all the arms of healing available. This includes, to name only a few, exercise, being in nature, my spiritual practice, Qi gong, plant allies, the right chemotherapy choices, the most experienced surgeon, the love from my ancestors, my family and friends. Heck, I'll take the love from strangers too :-).

I would not be where I am today without the support and love from all my friends and family. You love me unconditionally and that still blows my mind. I'm petulant, moody, bitchy, selfish and more. But you show up for me despite it all. Thank you for your forgiveness. Your good thoughts and prayers have fortified me. I'm (not really) ready for this next fight (I've come to accept that I can say I'm fighting cancer...i'm tired of befriending it), but here I am. I'm standing at the foot of yet another mountain, accompanied by your whispers of love and encouragement, which I will call on time and again. The words Thank You seem so small compared to the gratitude I feel.

I close this letter with words from a fellow cancer fighter, Cody. We had surgery around the same time, same chemo treatment and almost the same recurrence. He expresses what I feel. He is much better with words than I am.

I am living and dying with cancer. I disagree with the premise that the two realities are mutually exclusive. I can grieve and celebrate, prepare and live in the moment, accept others' grief as love and still enjoy life with them. I don't want to pretend, to choose in such a way that denies hope or reality. I don't want to lock myself or my loved ones into deception. Part of living is crying together. I am not afraid of grief. I am afraid of loss. I don't want to be lost in cancer. I want it to be an honest part of my life not the whole of it, nor to pretend it's not hanging around planning nasty stuff.

All of the above is subject to temporary reversal. Sometimes I want to be distracted, sometimes I want to wallow.

I hate that there is much I can no longer do, but I can love and be loved. To love and be loved is what we're here to learn, after all.

With love and gratitude,

Leslye Mukti
p.s. I've added some names here because people have asked how I'm doing. If you don't want to receive the emails, please let me know. I'm not offended and I don't want to fill your inbox with anything you don't want. I have over 12,000 emails in my inbox so I know what inbox overwhelm is. If you're new to this and you want my past (very revealing and sometimes dark) emails about how

cancer has affected my life, let me know and I'll try to send them.

The clock is ticking and my appointment is just hours away and I'm getting nervous. Yikes!!!! Breathe deep, she tells herself.

April 29, 2021

Hello Friends,

I want to thank you for all the love and support you send this way. I never knew how real, how tangible, sending love and good wishes and prayers were. I would think about people who were ailing or having a procedure, or any number of things that could be going on for someone where I stopped, thought about them, and sent good wishes. I had no idea if those made it into the presence of the person. Being on the receiving end, I find the expression of the words create images for me...and if I think about it, I feel it. Someone mentioned something about healing elixir. I found a vessel to bring to UCSF tomorrow, labeled it healing elixir, and am visualizing all your good thoughts entering that vessel...to sit with me for the 4+ hours of the infusion. Thank you for the gift of your loving presence.

Oh, yes, the plan. Since I last wrote about the recurrence, I have learned more. The surgeon I spoke with today told me there is a lot of disease.....peritoneal carcinomatosis...and it was probably there in microscopic form after my surgery in 2019. The chemotherapy may have kept it at bay, but when I finished, it began to grow. In late November, the liquid biopsy turned positive. Covid was also rearing its huge head. I was conversing with another surgeon in San Diego but at some point, everything was shut down there...I definitely was not going to explore surgery with ICU beds full. I also felt okay despite the positive results. In early Feb, nothing showed on my MRI except some ascites. Had I been in contact with a surgeon who really understands this ugly disease, I would have immediately scheduled a laparoscopic look around to determine how much cancer was in there. Peritoneal disease is very good at hiding and doesn't show up in scans until it's too late. (Forgive me if I'm repeating myself....brain/memory isn't what it used to be).

So, here we are today. I'm starting a new chemotherapy combo today. It will include irinotecan, which could give my gI tract a very good clean out....often. We'll add a biologic, Avastin, a monoclonal antibody...a targeted therapy. It works by interfering with the process of angiogenesis which is the ability to build new blood vessels. Treating peritoneal disease with chemotherapy is hit or miss. Mostly miss. However, it can work to put the brakes on, if not kill it completely.

The goal is to have CRS/HIPEC surgery...the Mother of All Surgeries. The reason is this surgery has the potential to cure. It has been very successful for appendiceal cancers, both low grade and high grade. With colon cancer and small bowel cancer, it's not as successful. This doesn't mean no hope. The key is to get as much of the cancer out of the body as possible. Since a lot of the cancer is the size of grains of sand, it's a tedious job. And one needs the best surgeon and team as possible. Someone with a LOT of experience. I'm talking with, and possibly working with a surgeon in Baltimore. There is one I've talked to at Stanford and we liked him, but the one in Baltimore was so spot on with understanding this disease. He also gives me hope. While acknowledging extensive cancer, he feels we can remove it, as long as it's not in places that will affect quality of life.

Hearing words like "extensive disease" is like a punch in the stomach. Yet, it hasn't yet invaded some areas of my body. I still feel hopeful that we'll be able to get it out. Still, it's hard not to get depressed. I woke up at 3:30 and cried some of the stress away. I need to go to treatment today with the attitude that I'm strong, this journey is one step at a time.

For those of you who don't know, I fast for 4 days...before and during chemo in the hopes I'll have fewer side effects. My lovely, amazing, supportive, giving man could use some good, nourishing meals. I know many have offered to help in some way, and bringing a meal to Steve would be awesome...I know he thinks it's okay to just buy a burrito every now and again, but I'm concerned for his sustenance and would love if we could get two delicious vegetarian meals a week for this wonderful man. I don't know how much cooking I'll feel like doing...depends on how crappy I feel with the chemo. But certainly, 4 days every two weeks of fasting means I'm not looking at food.

Those of you who might care to send healing thoughts, light, imagining the drugs being dripped into my veins as strong against the cancer but gentle on the healthy cells, I'll be starting the IV at 3:30 and will be there, welcoming this into my body, for 4 hours. I'll be imagining your beautiful thoughts entering my body too. . .making it the warrior body you all see (and the one I'm trying to see. Thank you!!!

May 26, 2021

I've been watching the magnificent full moon eclipse and thought about you...imagining being out in open space, surrounded by trees and beautiful mountains, as the bright moon slowly gets covered in a shadow.,.with only a sliver of light shining from the top right edge. So beautiful and sacred.
Later today we head to SF for my third chemotherapy treatment. This time around it's a little rougher in every aspect. A lot of fatigue, hair loss, cramping. Lately I've been feeling deflated...I question why I'm doing this as the disease is incurable. I suppose if we can control it, or even shrink it, then it's worth it. I'll have scans in mid June to get a better picture of whether the chemo is working. They want to add another drug that is more targeted treatment but has potentially horrible side effects, like bowel perforation! I have no idea how it works and may hold off for awhile. Anyway, it might be an auspicious time for a chemo treatment on this full moon day...Buddha's Birthday, full lunar eclipse.

I don't know when dreaming about being anywhere but where I am right now changed. I wasn't always like this. I used to have strong desires to be traveling, though I'm not really an adaptable traveler. I'd fill my calendar with imaginary trips, never really content with being where I was.
Lately, the only place I felt a true need to be besides my home was Bali. Nathan and family live there so, besides being a great place to visit, I needed to be with my family.

However, even before my cancer diagnosis, I'd stopped planning trips around the world. I've been feeling content with being home. I love my home. There is a part of me that has felt I will die from this cancer. I can go into a long story about that, but what has been compelling me to write are the painful thoughts that have been going through my head as I played sudoku. Longing hits at such strange times.

Night is a fickle thing. Sleep teases you but worries also come to taunt you. It seems all the fears that have been dancing in the mind show up shamelessly loud in the night when everyone else is sleeping. The sadness you didn't already express the 40 times you broke down in tears earlier come up.

Tonight, the sadness of never returning to Bali again came to haunt me.

I thought I had come to a resolution that I wouldn't again take long distance trips. Having cancer during a pandemic really smacked my face hard with that reality. So, as one must do when accepting ones fate, I settled into knowing I wasn't going to go there again.

Tonight I was overtaken with a desire to once again plant myself smack onto the sacred island of Bali. I want to smell Bali again. I long to be at Nathan's home, hearing the roosters all day, the neighbors playing instruments and singing. I want to sit in a crowded car with my family while we drive on the impossibly narrow dirt roads crowded with other cars, trucks and motorbikes as we bump along to the beach. I want to sip coconut water out of large young coconuts the women hack open so easily with their machetes. I want to stop at *Pepito* on the way home while the kids are sandy and tired, waiting in the car as we run in for snacks. I want to play with my grandchildren before we eat dinner, shower and go to sleep. I want to once again walk outside and down the stairs into the main house to pee several times through the night. Poor Steve snoring and hot in the bed we share because I can't stand the A/C at night. My longing to be there is stronger than ever. Is this grasping for something I'll never experience again happening because my hope for living for a few more years is waning? Is this what is going to happen? The peace that I thought I'd feel, that I've worked so hard to cultivate is thrown out the window as the reality of the end of my life nears? Maybe it's part of the process. Maybe it is presenting so I can grieve what I thought I'd already grieved. Maybe it's happening so letting go will be easier. I don't know. I just know that as I think about Bali…the food, the ceremonies, the road trips, the noise, the music, the bugs, the beauty, the smiles, the glares, Puakan, barongs, smells, rice fields, friends, family, monkeys, glued to Steve as we adventure, Nathan, Sari, Sri, my grandchildren, magic…I am filled with longing to once more be there. Maybe because my last trip there I felt so bad I spent most of the 6 weeks laying on any bed I could find. Ah, tonight my heart hurts a little more. There are hard lumps in my throat as I try not to cry. My back hurts and I think is this the beginning of the end… and writing my feelings has helped me process a little more. And you, my love, sleep restlessly next to me. What are you dreaming of that is creating such restless sleep? I want to elbow you often because your breathing is again stopping. But I don't. I now know it will start again. But if I count past 60 and you haven't taken a breath, it's so tempting. Then that thought creeps into my brain…who is going to make sure you're breathing at night? Who is going to startle you on long car trips so you get a nice adrenaline rush that will keep you awake. Maybe, like so many movies we watch, I'll still be there in some form or another "protecting" you (I say "protecting" because I'm sure you don't see it like that... it's more like "abusing")   But you know it's because I love you.

June 20, 2021

Hello Dear Group,

I wanted to share this letter BhavanI had shared at one of the online retreats...I asked her to please send it to me as it was so beautiful and resonated with me when she read it.

I occasionally write updates as to my treatments. I've had an email group since my diagnosis, so a few of you have been receiving this for awhile now. I must admit that it is not only an update on the treatment, but often a window into my twisted and confused mind :-), which means it's not always uplifting. I usually sit down and write when I feel the need, and not being a "writer," it is often a stream of consciousness type of thing, expressing thoughts running through my mind as I experience living and dying with cancer.

I felt compelled to write this morning as I have scans coming up tomorrow and I anticipate a lot of decisions making this coming week.

Happy Summer Solstice. It feels somehow comforting that I will be getting scans on the Solstice. The longest day...honoring the light within...that light within all of us.

Much, much love,
Mukti

Letter from Babaji

The real cave is your own heart. The main idea is to search inside, but it's not so easy because the mind is distracted by objects. It never works, to find happiness from outer objects. Because everything is changing, mortal, and unreal. Look inside and go on piercing the darkness and you will find light.

*Understand your desire to live and fear to die.
As soon as you understand it, there is neither life nor death. You will be in perfect peace.
A peace which will never wear out, which will never get dim or eliminated.
It's a flame of peace,
unaffected by the wind of desires.*

*To attain that peace, you walk through a very narrow lane of nonattachment.
In that lane only one can walk. It's a lane for lonely seekers of light and love.
Alone which is constant and inexhaustible.
Call it peace, truth, God – it doesn't matter.*

June 20, 2021

First thoughts...Thank you for being with me on this strange journey. There are some people reading this who I've actually never met in person, yet you have continued to offer healing prayers and thoughts. I don't know how I deserve such love, but Thank you! I've bared my crazy self to you all, written about my childhood to my struggle with self loathing/self love, to this surreal experience with cancer and mortality. You didn't know what you were getting when I offered updates on this illness. Truthfully, I didn't know what was going to come out of my mouth....I mean my head via these fingers....when I began sharing about having cancer. If I think back, it's embarrassing, sort of, to be so open, to reveal myself like this. I both apologize and thank you for riding along with me. I'm not offended if you tell me you've had enough, if you want off this list. I imagine as this disease progresses, these updates will get more ugly, more painful and it might not be what you want to read, so I take no offense if this isn't your jam.

I finished my 4th chemotherapy treatment. This chemo combo is hard on my body. I feel very fatigued for days and days and days. I might begin feeling better a few days before I go back to the infusion center. I'm not used to this type of fatigue where I cannot make my body go for a walk. I literally have to force myself to get my shoes on and make these legs move. Imagine a stubborn dog being forced to walk away from something it is enjoying. Because I'm also in quite a fog mentally, I have to have some company. I seriously don't trust myself crossing the busy street these days. This healing potion (I'm trying so hard not to call it the poison that it is) affects the body in unexpected ways. It's another lesson in acceptance...acceptance of loss of mental acuity, (you can probably see it in my writing), loss of hair, loss of bodily comfort, loss of energy. It's hard to distinguish what might be side effects from chemo or what might be the cancer impacting my organs. I hope and pray it's doing what it's supposed to do....make those rogue cancer cells that have hijacked pathways to life ...experience mortality.

Which brings me to tomorrow. Tomorrow I get an MRI and CT scan to see if this treatment is working. Systemic chemotherapy typically doesn't work well on peritoneal disease. The cancer is more like a layer of frosting on a cake (don't let this image repulse you next time you eat cake), spreading all over the inside of my abdominal cavity, covering the various organs that live in there. Imagine those little colorful sprinkles on frosting...those are the cancer cells. We're not attacking a big tumor, but 1000's of small ones. While some people don't respond to systemic chemotherapy, others do. It could depend on mutations. No one knows. The other reason we're going this route is the aggressive signet ring cell. My doctors want to make sure we're stopping any potential cancer growth in the lungs or liver. Luckily it's not showing up there, but my surgeon says he doesn't trust scans with mucinous signet ring cell cancer. Tomorrow I face, for the first time, getting scans to see if there is progression or stability of disease. When I had chemotherapy last year, it was considered "clean up" chemo...used to kill any cells that surgery missed, or, because there were so many lymph nodes positive for cancer, anything that might be traveling in my system. Progressing to stage 4, all images from here onward are to see if the treatment is working to keep the cancer "stable." I remember when I was first diagnosed, the oncologist told me chemotherapy for stage 3 could be curative and chemotherapy for stage 4 was palliative. Those words haunt me. Needless to say, getting scans now creates strong feelings of anxiety. This probably explains why my emotions are like a pinball in a machine, ricocheting here, there, everywhere. I can feel fine stepping into the shower and suddenly, I'm a sobbing mess...tears falling down my face harder than the water pelting down on my body.

Many of you might have seen that beautiful video of the young woman, Nightbirde, singing on that talent show [*America's Got Talent*] (if not, I suggest watching it). She is living with stage 4 cancer. At one point she says, "You can't wait until life isn't hard anymore before you decide to be happy." While that is very true, it's not possible to be happy all the time. I'm guessing she knows that too. Perhaps happiness is bigger than we know. Maybe the feelings of sadness, grief, fear fall under the big umbrella of happiness. Yes, I think that must be the case. What she says is very true...and I think many of us facing death (who isn't facing death?...it's just those of us with terminal illness are more aware of this reality) find our lives changed so much that there is a conscious letting go of thoughts and actions that don't serve us. There is a letting in of the love that surrounds us, of finally ALLOWING that love, of believing we're worthy of that love. There is also allowing ourselves to express love to others in ways we might not have in the past. Well, I can't say this is true for everyone, and I'm certainly not suggesting a Pollyanna view of illness. But this is something I have experienced.

Oh, where did my mind wander now? I was saying I'm scared about the test results. What if the cancer progressed? How will I handle the news? What will the next steps be? Will I want to go there? I'll tell you some of the things I know. My oncologist says we have some "tools in the toolbox." We haven't exhausted our options yet. My surgeon will be scrutinizing the results to decide if I'm a candidate for CRS/HIPEC surgery. First he'll do an exploratory laparoscopy to see the extent of the cancer because, as I mentioned, it's hard to see what's really going on with imaging. If the cancer isn't too extensive, surgery will be an option. I've got mixed feelings about this surgery as there can be many post surgical complications.

It's a long recovery. Yet, if the surgery can give some extended quality of life, it just might be worth it. I live in the unknown right now. It is humbling to live with so much uncertainty...it is challenging and perhaps it also helps develop resilience...resilience and acceptance. For a control freak, this is not easy.

I have so many thoughts about life and death, but that will probably be in another update as my butt is hurting from sitting. One little thought about death.....it has been almost two years that I've been looking at that thin veil...tiptoeing to the edge of the cliff with eyes wide open (not willingly, by the way). This has given me some time to try to find peace in the fact that we're all going to die one day, and my time is closer than I once imagined. Of course, it could be closer still as anyone can experience a sudden, unexpected death. This disease has brought the reality of death into my daily thoughts. I am grateful for every day I wake up....another day to learn, another day to connect with my family and friends, another day to live and practice non-attachment (definitely not as easy as the enlightened ones make it sound), another day to just BE. Yes, like Nightbirde says, "You can't wait until life isn't hard anymore before you decide to be happy." Even when I'm curled in a ball, crying my eyes out, I believe this. I welcome all the emotions that come with being a human...to deny them would not be fully living (for me).

This coming week will be stepping into new territory for me and my family. I feel comforted knowing I'm held by so many as I walk this lonely road. I know you are by our side, and as Ram Dass said, **"We are all just walking each other home."**

I feel you, I hope you feel me, here, together, always, in Love.

In gratitude,
Leslye Mukti

June 27, 2021

Hello,
I wanted to send an update after my scans last week. The good news is the cancer doesn't appear to be growing. They say the cancer is looking stable. Stable is good!! I was so afraid I was going to hear that it has grown and we need a new plan. The side effects are hard after the treatment and it makes me think it's the cancer growing. From what the doctors told me this week, it's most likely just the side effects from the treatments. One big clue is that the pain stops after some days. So this is a great thing.

We were disappointed when talking to the surgeon because he was not encouraging about getting the surgery. Honestly, that surgery scares me and I don't know how I would feel if I were eligible for it. I understand that surgery is most likely the only way all the cancer could be removed from my body. However, it's a risky surgery and the success rate with colon cancer is not the same as appendix cancer. That said, I've "met" people in my support groups that have had the cancer and, while it did recur, they're still around, albeit on chemotherapy.

The plan is to continue with the chemotherapy for another 4 cycles (two months), have scans again, and see what the surgeon thinks. It's a strange thing...to see my future in 2-3 month increments.

However, I'll take that over having a surprise complication from the cancer any day!

We were so happy to finally get to meet the oncologist in person. It really makes a difference to meet face to face with the person who is helping fight this disease. She is smart, compassionate and listens to our concerns.

I think I've mentioned this before, but I have an oncologist in Ohio who Steve and I both love!! He is so caring and smart. I consult over video with him every month. If he had a different opinion on my treatment, I'd pack my bags and move there. So far he agrees with the plan. One reason I value his opinion so much, besides his big heart, is he is part of a group that is studying signet ring cell cancer. It is so rare for colon cancer to have this histology, there is not a lot known about it. I'm finding out that having a rare cancer really limits treatment options so it's awesome to find the one place in all the United States that is studying this disease.

I have so much gratitude for this community of ours. Thank you!! I am just one of many you all support and love, and I know so many have their own hardships to deal with. We are a lucky tribe, being held in so much love and support. Thank you for allowing me to share my slice of life with you.

Tomorrow is treatment #5. Gonna visualize that chemotherapy going after the cancer cells...stopping any growth...and seeing big shrinkage of what is there. As always, I'll be bringing my reminders of your support with me.

Much, much love and gratitude.

August 29, 2021

Greetings,

An update is long overdue and so much has happened!! Yet......

I went through a period of questioning my writing. In fact, I felt embarrassed for everything I've written over these past two years. My mind went to some dark places and for some reason, I had no filters and spewed my entire insides, my childhood challenges, my insecurities, everything! Yikes....and some of you on this list have never met me in person. Yet you send me so much love and support. It means so much to me...and I wish there was a way I could give back all that I've received. I also want to remind you that I will not be offended in any way whatsoever if you don't want to receive the emails. It's not always pretty...so please let me know if you want off this ride. :-)

Two years! It's been almost two years since my diagnosis. September 10th is the day we found out about cancer. The very strange thing is I feel soooooo good today, Two years ago, before I knew I had cancer, I felt like I was dying. I'd been sick for months and had no idea what was going on. I'd lost so much weight, had zero energy, had pain in my upper abdomen and back, and just had no life energy. The irony of feeling so good now, while I'm living with a scary cancer that is growing in the lining of my abdomen and on many organs, is just crazy! I could almost pretend I don't have cancer (until I get a headache and it doesn't go away, so I must have brain mets, or my leg is hurting so I must have one of those infamous blood clots, or things moving through my intestine hurt so I must have a blockage...you get the idea).

Two years ago, I was withdrawing from life. I still remember feeling like a ghost walking in this world. Perhaps I was practicing for death. I witnessed life going on without me. Of course, we're all going to have that experience one day...but I was living into it every day.
I remember attending a New Year's retreat online. I cried so hard after the beautiful New Year's ceremony. It was a moving experience, even online. I cried because thought, wow, this is my last one! It's weird living with a terminal disease because the shadow of death is always present. People ask me how long I'll be on chemo because when it was stage 3, there was a plan. The plan was 6 months of chemotherapy and then it's finished. With stage 4 cancer, chemotherapy is not finished. The art is to have enough chemo to keep the cancer from growing (and hopefully shrink it) but not so much that it kills important organs, like the heart or lungs. It's a fine balancing act to keep the body healthy while infusing it with poison. If the chemo doesn't kill the cancer, then hopefully it will keep it from growing until there is a better treatment.That is why I'm so thankful for the two oncologists I have. They are artists, thinkers, not stuck in a standard of care treatment box. They haven't told me to go home and call hospice because nothing can be done. Believe me, there are oncologists who tell this to their patients. I feel blessed every day to have met such smart, compassionate, and dedicated oncologists.

Now I'm meeting skilled surgeons. Surgeons who will open someone up and search for every last drop of cancer that is growing inside the abdomen. Every last drop of visible cancer. I can't imagine what kind of training a surgeon has to go through to have that kind of eye. The surgery will remove any organs covered with cancer (the organs one can survive without) and then scrape and scrape the cancer away. For example, we know from the scans that there is cancer living on my diaphragm, spleen, parts of my liver, on my omentum, and the bottom of my pelvis. Scans are far from perfect from detecting what is really going on. Sometimes the cancer they see could actually be "dead" cancer...something the chemo killed (I'm still trying to understand all this). Sometimes there is much more cancer inside the abdomen but can't be seen on scans because it's too small or in places that won't show up. There are people who had clear scans, but when they went in for, say, surgery for a hernia, cancer was discovered all over the inside of the abdominal area. This is NOT the surgery I'm getting right now. It is one of the possibilities we could be looking at in the next couple of months.

On Wednesday, Sept 1st, I am having a diagnostic laparoscopy to get a definitive assessment of what is going on inside me. There is a scale of measurement used to determine if someone is eligible for the cytoreductive surgery and HIPEC (heated chemo piped in after all the visible cancer is removed, and kept there for 1.5 hours so it can kill any microscopic cells left over). Once we find out, I'll have some major decisions to make. The big surgery, aptly nicknamed the mother of all surgeries (MOAS), has a possibility of a lot of post surgical complications and a very long recovery period. It's also not as effective for colon cancer as it is for appendiceal or ovarian cancer. In fact, one of the surgeons I talked to thought I may not benefit from it because I have that rare signet ring cell cancer. I've consulted with two other surgeons who feel differently, telling me that signet ring cell comes in all different flavors. I guess we'll have more answers after Wednesday. And guess what. I'm terrified of the diagnostic laparoscopy. If I'm this scared of a 1-2 hour surgery, I'm really going to have to dig deeply to find the courage to have another...if I'm even eligible.

So, I'm asking for support from my community. My surgery is scheduled for 4pm on 9/1, pacific time. It could be as early as 2 pm, depending on if Dr. L.... finishes his other cases early. It would mean so much to me if you could send some good vibes my way. I like to imagine the surgical team having a restful night, a stress free day, a morning free of conflict, and enthusiasm for the procedure. I also imagine 100's of hands accompanying me in the OR. I am trying hard to see myself on the other end of surgery....awake, with the incisions healing quickly. I really am a wimp!!! People say I'm strong, but I'm not. I'm scared. I think of my brave beautiful mom who endured so many surgeries in her life. I think of her amazing courage as she faced breast cancer in her 40's and then leukemia 18 years later, which took her life.
So, we're off to San Diego tomorrow morning. I'll fill you all in on what was found with the laparoscopy and what the possible next steps are sometime after our return.

Much, much love and appreciation,
Leslye/Mukti

September 2, 2021

Hello All,

It's over...yay!!! I'm so happy to be on the recovering side of surgery.

All went exceedingly well!! Thank you for all your well wishes, prayers, love. I know that holding me in your heart, sending strong prayers and accompanying me in spirit during this procedure has made all the difference in the world. Thank you, Thank you, Thank you!!

I got a call from the hospital that the surgeon was running ahead of schedule and my surgery was going to be 2 hours earlier. Woo hoo! It was definitely going to be a challenge not drinking water the entire day.

Arriving at the hospital, there was a group of anti-maskers, anti-vaxxers, Governor-recall supporters, those who believe the presidential election was stolen, having a rally. Incensed about vaccines yet also unwilling to wear a mask because it takes away their freedom (to spread their germs), they were spouting hatred. Definitely NOT something I needed to walk by as I entered the hospital for surgery. I'm a proponent for free speech, but this was the wrong place at the wrong time. This got me super agitated as I was hoping for a sense of calm and harmony on surgery day. I didn't want my team rattled by all this hatred and conflict. Perhaps they weren't. I'm a very sensitive person and have a hard time putting up a protective shield.

Anyway....my surgical team Is AWESOME. Funny, talkative, kind, understanding of my fears. They ask so many questions during pre-op. One of them was what were my expectations to get out of surgery. Hmmmm....no problem answering that one. "I want to come out the other end alive."

After having to clean the body again with something that made some parts of my skin break out (had to shower twice with it prior to arrival), I also had to brush and rinse with something and then clean my nostrils twice with iodine looking stuff. No blowing the nose, so it kept dripping out and made my nose get stuffy. The young and kind anesthesiologist told me it's no problem that I can't really breathe out of my nose because they put a tube down your throat to do the breathing for you (and I've got a sore throat as proof).

After all that, I was wheeled to the OR where the surgical team was waiting. On the way, I asked the anesthesiologist where was the "happy juice" I'd heard about. If you know me, you know I take a Valium before most procedures, like an MRI, getting dental work done, or before my chemo infusions. I need the calming down that provides. I told him I needed that happy juice while I was in the waiting room, nervously pinching the crystal I brought and pacing the halls and going up and down the stairs I found. Idid not take Valium in the morning. I couldn't believe I was facing this without the help of an anti-anxiety drug or the " happy juice" I'd heard I'd get!

The competent and humorous team got to work moving me to the smaller table, strapping me down, and getting ready for action. I couldn't believe I was experiencing this unassisted by my needed antianxiety medication. But, hey, Idid it and it was fine! Suddenly knowing I was about to have my abdomen explored to determine the extent of cancer invasion, was going to be cut and blown up with gas, was going to have this body get drugs that would slow it down and make me unconscious, I started crying (see, that's what happens without antianxiety drugs...I feel all my emotions). As the anesthesiologist put the oxygen mask over my face and asked me to breathe deeply (sort of a hard task when one is crying), my surgeon came over and held my hand. His soft, skilled hand that would be working on my body reached out for mine, with such gentleness, making me feel cared for as I slipped away, slowly losing consciousness. I remember thinking I'm really doing this…and then, by some saving grace, began chanting Ram (a Hindu deity) in my head.

Next thing I know, I'm in the recovery room. My surgeon told me it went great. The best news he said was there was LESS disease than he expected to find!!! LESS cancer! One of my biggest fears was hearing I was riddled with cancer. It's not unfounded because this is often the case with peritoneal carcinomatosis. Especially when signet ring cells are found in the tumors. The scary and sad stories I'd heard of people with this disease, who completed chemo and had clear scans, then had hernia repair surgery, only to find their insides were covered in disease, is not uncommon.

If I decide to get the CRS/HIPEC, it may mean an easier recovery (well, open abdominal surgery isn't easy, but relative to mist HIPEC surgeries) and, at this point, no organs removed. No organs removed is a big deal!! I'll have the omentum removed because mist of the cancer is covering that and something else that I can't remember right now.

I wanted to share the good news with you all!!! You have been on this journey with me and have helped me so much!! I didn't think I'd be here right now, writing these words to you!!!

I sign off with loads of gratitude and love.

September 2, 2021

I had the diagnostic laparoscopy yesterday and the news is better than anyone expected!

The surgeon said there was less disease than he expected. Also, it's not covering organs so, from what he saw, I wouldn't need organs to be removed. That could make CRS a little easier and possibly fewer post surgical complications.

I'm really happy with this result, especially knowing I have a certain histology that could make this look different.

So I won't be a wreck, crying my eyes out, feeling hopeless when I talk you...instead I want to send a cake and party hats!!

Anyway just wanted to update you.

October 14, 2021

It's amazing how quickly time passes, yet when I think back to September 1st, it seems it was a lifetime ago.

September 1st was the day I had the diagnostic laparoscopy that was to change the direction of my life. That was the day I found out there was less disease inside my body than the surgeon expected. That was the day I was told I was a candidate for cytoreductive surgery (CRS). That was the day I should have been thrilled. From that day onward, I've lived in terror. Suddenly, I was waking up every morning, realizing the course of treating this disease had taken a turn, a turn towards a procedure I never thought would have. I found myself consumed with thoughts of this surgery...what it entailed, what could go wrong, how I might feel afterwards, am I hastening my trajectory towards death. I could treat the disease with months of chemotherapy rather than be cut and scraped and then having heated chemotherapy piped into my abdominal cavity for 90 minutes. This surgery has the nickname, MOAS, or Mother of All Surgeries. Recovery is rough, according to many people who had it. Some were in the hospital for 30-45 days as post surgical complications hit one after the other. Many had scary, near death experiences. There were also the few that had easy recoveries, feeling somewhat normal 6-8 weeks post surgery. But the scary stories had a much louder voice in my head.

I'd known about CRS as many people with my type of cancer had gotten this surgery. In fact, I'd been encouraged to have a 'diagnostic lap' for months and months. The biology of my particular tumor is such that it tends to metastasize to the peritoneum. In fact, because it had grown through the intestinal wall, it had already been touching the lining of my abdomen, and had already implanted some cancer cells in the mesentery, which were removed with my original surgery.

If you recall from previous emails, the liquid biopsy that detects circulating cancer cells had gone from negative to positive in November, 2020. I asked my surgeon to please take a look. She said there was always a risk when doing surgery, and the only option would be CRS/HIPEC surgery, and perhaps I should wait until there was clinical evidence before moving forward with that. I'd had an MRI in January, 2021, looking for clinical evidence of disease as that is what informs a treatment plan. Nothing showed up on my scans other than some ascites. That should have been an indicator to have the diagnostic surgery, but it wasn't suggested. It wasn't until April that the cancer showed on scans. That was when I began the new chemotherapy regime. That chemo was harder on my body in some ways than the first line of chemo treatment I'd had. The intention was now to watch for shrinkage of the cancer so I could possibly have surgery. We scanned every 2 months. After the first scan, I was told by a surgeon that I was not a very good candidate for this surgery. The cancer was not shrinking, but it also was not growing. He told me because I have the rare but aggressive signet ring cell, and because I was on a reduced dose of one of the chemotherapy drugs, I probably wouldn't be eligible for this surgery. The risk was not worth the benefit. While I didn't really want this surgery, I guess there was a part of me that did, as getting cancer removed from the body can be a curative treatment. So, feeling quite depressed, I continued the chemotherapy. Two months later another scan showed the cancer was staying stable. It wasn't shrinking, but it wasn't growing. Because of that, I was able to have the diagnostic surgery with my new surgeon in San Diego that would ultimately change the course of my treatment. My oncologist told me if I was entertaining the thought of CRS, even a little bit, it would behoove me to have the diagnostic lap.

After finding out I was a candidate, I wanted to hear that this surgery was the best choice for me. I wanted my oncologist to jump for joy, to tell me how lucky I was that I was eligible, to tell me, YES, YES do this surgery. She remained neutral, telling me I'd been wanting to seek alternatives to standard of treatment. She told me I could continue on chemo for some time. She didn't see imminent death. She informed me that typically, people with peritoneal carcinomatosis lived a median of 2 years, but that was just a number. I asked, what would you tell your mother if she was in my situation...I was fishing for answers but she didn't bite. I wanted someone to tell me what to do, but I was left with weighing the facts. So I wrote to my surgeon and asked him why he thought I was a good candidate. He told me, in very few words, "Because we think we can remove all the cancer, it's as simple as that." Removing all the cancer! Removing all the cancer...that is the goal for any cancer patient.

I'd consulted with two more surgeons, both who told me if I was eligible for CRS, that would be the best course of action for me. One of the surgeons was running a clinical trial on bromelain and acetylcysteine being injected into the abdomen, essentially dissolving the mucinous tumors. However, it was a treatment aimed at people who were not candidates for surgery. In case you don't know, cutting cancer from the body is the goal most people shoot for. It's the reason many people do chemotherapy. Getting cancer small enough to cut it out from your liver or any organ that previously couldn't be touched is a curative intention. Many people are not given an option to get the cancer removed and are simply put on palliative chemotherapy...sometimes years of it. Cancer is often treated as a chronic disease. But cancer becomes resistant to those drugs, so it becomes a game of whack-a-mole. Getting to the point of surgery, where the cancer can be removed, hopefully for good, is what one really wants. But surgery is scary!!!!! Especially this MOAS!!!

Another surgeon told me I'm a good candidate for this surgery because:

1) the amount of disease is within the scope of a successful complete removal of all visible cancer.

2) Despite the odds, my cancer did not spread systemically (knock on wood). Two years have passed and it is not in my lungs or liver. This is a GOOD sign. I had 14 lymph nodes with cancer in them and a tumor that penetrated the intestine and implanted in the peritoneum. Most likely my metastasis is due to that.

3) The disease is not on my small intestine, or any organs that will need to be removed, therefore it will be a less radical surgery.

4) There must be a #4 and 5 but I can't remember them.

He said despite the signet ring cell, all these things pointed to a successful surgery.

All this is GOOD! Yet I cry almost every morning. I cry at random times throughout the day. Each day that passes brings me closer to October 20th, the day I have this surgery. I can't tell you how many times I wanted to say NO...NO, I'm not doing this!! But what are my alternatives? They are; to stay on this very strong chemotherapy for as long as it works (how long that is, no one knows), then try other chemotherapies until they no longer work, then do clinical trials. I'd risk the cancer growing over other organs and causing life threatening complications. Also, if there is more disease inside, I lose the opportunity to have the cancer removed. I know all roads eventually lead to death (isn't that the path for all of us?). I've spent the last two years making peace with this. Covid has made these last two years painfully lonely. The vaccine allowed get togethers with friends, hugs, carpooling, camping together, sleeping in a tent with my daughter, meals and game nights with friends, etc. There was more normalcy again because the risk of getting infected by a virus, especially having a compromised immune system, was minimized tremendously. At least I wasn't going to die in isolation. My heart hurts for all the people who had to die alone.

I have a tendency to see *Worst Case Scenarios* in everything. It's a horrible side effect of growing up with childhood trauma. It's something I've been working on eliminating, but it's not so easy....the taproot runs deep and is hard to remove. It's been a struggle to change my mindset. Since having cancer and knowing I had to have strong (poisonous) drugs, I stopped reading about side effects. I now sign consent forms without reading them. Even with the herbal protocol, I stopped researching. I used to research every herb I took...looking for possible dangers, being prepared. I didn't do that with my herbal protocol and experienced some nasty side effects from one particular herb that I had to stop taking. So, I ride the Worst Case Scenario bus....I ride it when I have scans, I ride it when I take drugs, I ride it when I need simple procedures (this bus is what kept me from having a colonoscopy all my life...the 1% of people who get a perforated colon and die...*don't make the same mistake as I did*), I ride it when I need surgery. Learning to stay off that bus is not easy. I want off that bus and don't want to get back on it.

I've spent the last 4 weeks preparing for surgery. I'm trying to get more protein (it's very hard to get 45-55 grams of protein as a vegetarian), trying to get more exercise (but 4 weeks have passed and I still haven't started weight training), and I've gotten many tests, including another colonoscopy.

PSA....get your colon checked! Especially if you have pain, bloating, blood, irregular bowel movements...a colonoscopy is so much easier than chemotherapy, surgery and the close proximity of death).

My colonoscopy was clear and there was no growth of cancer at the site of the reconnection from my first surgery. That is great because often that is a place cancer grows back and then I would need more colon removed with this upcoming surgery...and that just adds to more possible complications. My mammogram was clear, so no breast cancer (this is what runs in my family). I was tested for the penicillin allergy I grew up thinking I had due to a reaction I had when I was 3. I am not allergic to penicillin, which means the surgeon has more options if I develop an infection post surgery. I just had an abdominal MRI today to check for any cancer growth as I've been off chemotherapy for a month. If those results are good, surgery is a go. The surgeon will first take a look inside with a small incision to look for disease progression before cutting my belly further. If no progression is seen, he will proceed with cutting my belly from the chest to the pubic bone and proceed with the tedious procedure of removing all visible cancer. As it is, I have disease on my diaphragm, some spots on my liver, and some disease in the right side of my pelvis. The omentum also has cancer on it so it will be removed. Luckily, no organs will have to be removed, although I'm getting the ovaries out as cancer often metastasizes to those little things.

We will be heading to San Diego on Saturday. We had to purchase a vehicle that we could sleep in (which we did when I had the diagnostic lap last month), and one that was reliable for long distance travel. We will stay with Steve's uncle Saturday night (he and his wife have been such a wonderful support to me...very nurturing and encouraging and loving) and uncertain about Sunday night right now. We rented an airbnb that is right near the hospital for the first week and then a new friend generously offered her condo for the next 3 weeks. If all goes well, I will only be in the hospital for 7-10 days. We will need to stay nearby for post op visits. My daughter will come down to be there during my surgery and for a week or so afterwards. She is a wonderful advocate and will make sure I get everything I need from the hospital staff. Steve, of course, will be there 24/7. This man is amazing. I don't know how I got so incredibly lucky to have this man in my life. He has been by my side, literally, these past two years. From driving to every single doctor appointment, every chemo appointment, sleeping in a chair during my first surgery 2 years ago, being my rock while I ride the roller coaster of emotions....I just can't say enough about what this beautiful man has done. I don't know where he finds the fortitude to do all he does. He has an unflappable nature, which has been just what I need. Perhaps his 30 years of working with small children has given him patience and equanimity. Maybe he really, really, really does love me and I better wake up to that fact! I am incredibly blessed.

I have the best support system in the world. I feel sad that for some people, having cancer means people disappear from their lives. I understand it's hard to watch someone suffer, it's hard to feel helpless and not be able to fix the situation and that makes people shy away. It is hard to just BE with someone, being okay with not being able to fix the situation. I know....I've been there! I am sad that I was not as good a friend to the important people in my life who experienced loss. It hurt me knowing there was nothing I could do to take away the pain. I didn't know that it was OKAY to simply say, "I don't know what to do, but I love you and I'm right here." What a powerful lesson. I still struggle with that as I've met so many people with cancer through my online support and have been there as some of them reached the end of the road of this life.

The love and acceptance I have felt, the heart to heart connections, the concern, the generosity, the offerings of support and love, the kind words, the ability to just be with me...I've learned so much. I have the BEST family ever! Both my family and Steve's family have been with me in ways I never imagined. So have my friends...both near and distant. Why did it take getting sick for me to realize how much people care? I'm sad for the walls I had constructed but I'm glad they are breaking down. I hope my love for you all is felt by you. I don't like being a "taker" because I like to give. It has been humbling to be in this situation and be a receiver. I have learned to ask for what I need (to a certain extent), and it has been met with open arms and open hearts. Words simply cannot express the gratitude I feel. My heart is full and that gives me peace. I hope I share the feeling of love with you all and that you feel some peace in your hearts too. Before you think I'm just embracing bliss all the time, please know that I'm still the grumpy, bossy, controlling, bitchy person I always was. Perhaps it's just a little tempered. I guess one can live with all the things we want to work on eliminating, but accepting they still arise, AND live with feeling loved and loving back. Being human...such a complicated structure. I am not blind to the suffering of the world, the suffering of my friends and family, the suffering of the animals, the trees, the water, our mother earth, the hatred between people.....no, I'm not. I have not lost my desire to participate in building bridges. Yes, I'm caught up in my disease and facing death, yet I still deeply care for the world I live in, for the pain my friends and family experience, and all that. My problem is small in comparison, but I don't like to compare. So, please know I am here to meet you wherever you are....don't think you can't share your pains, your sorrows with me. I am here, I hear you, I see you, I love you. I love YOU!!! And, ITHANK YOU from the depths of my heart.

(if there is anyone I left out, I apologize...I am pretty spaced out and preoccupied lately. Feel free to share the news with my friends if they want to receive such news. I know at times it's been pretty dark, but that is my truth. As usual, I invite anyone who no longer wishes to receive these updates to let me know. I hate sending unwanted emails. I am not offended if you don't wish to receive them. And if someone wants them and i've left them off, please give them my email address so I can add them. xoxoxoxoxo)

October 28, 2021

I learned that things don't always turn out the way you planned, or the way you think they should. And I've learned that there are things that go wrong that don't always get fixed or get put back together the way they were before. I've learned that some broken things stay broken, and I've learned that you can get through bad times and keep looking for better ones, as long as you have people who love you. - Jennifer Weiner

I've been meaning to write an update but haven't had a clear head. It's 1:30 am and I can't sleep. Perhaps a little writing will help clear some things out and allow the sleep to bathe me, from the top of my nearly hairless head, down to my dried and peeling feet.

I am still reeling from the shock of waking in the recovery room, and hearing my surgeon telling me they didn't proceed with the surgery. It was a very surreal moment, though very foggy in my memory.

As you all know, I was terrified to have this surgery and questioned my intention many times. I knew the potential was there to get this cancer out and possibly be free of disease for quite some time. I knew we had a small window of opportunity and I needed to act quickly. I spent 5 weeks, waking up almost every morning in tears, as I never thought I would consent to having a procedure quite like this. Yet, I committed and the last week we were in Santa Cruz, we prepared to go. We cleaned our house as one does when expecting a baby (that good old nesting feeling), packed photos, prayer beads, crystals, cards people sent, positive affirmations for healing that my family drew to hang in the hospital room, clean sheets to sleep in the night before surgery, food and clothes. Our plumbing line broke one night so we waited until 1am for the emergency plumber to come...which never happened until 8:30 the next morning. Our "new to us van" needed a major repair (when it rains, it pours). We paid bills in advance. I filled out an advance directive, visited with friends, and tried to prepare myself for what was ahead. We headed down to San Diego in 2 days, staying with Steve's uncle and his wife the first night (they have been so welcoming and comforting to me and fills a need to have that feeling of parental family love) and some new friends we'd just met the second night, who took such good care of us while we were with them.

I got my covid test the day we arrived and got my labs done. The second day we met with the surgeon for last minute check in, found out my insurance was not covering a portion of the surgery, and signed all sorts of consent forms. We picked my daughter up at the airport that evening and I took the 2 showers required, cleaning with a very antibacterial scrub they give you pre surgery. I drank the yucky high carb drinks (for anyone who hasn't had surgery in awhile, this is a new thing that is supposed to help with a faster recovery...carbo load the body), took a valium and tried to sleep. I had to wake at 3:30 to drink another bottle of the high carb drink and shower again with the stinging antibacterial soap.

We tearfully headed to the hospital, checked in and had to once again scrub my entire body with pads of antibacterial scrubs, clean my nostrils with iodine, brush and gargle with some strong antibacterial rinse and wait nervously for operating time. The doctors and nurses were so kind, especially the doctor who came to put an epidural in my upper back. I was so scared to get that inserted, but it didn't hurt. Getting the IV line in my little veins is always an adventure and the blood likes to gush out when poked, so the nice white sheets had a little pool of red as I lay there. I just stared at that red spot as I lay there waiting. That's about all I remember. Until that haunting moment in the recovery room.

I remember waking up in the recovery room and looking at the clock. 10:45 AM. I asked if they got all the cancer out and if I received the HIPEC (the hot chemo they put in after removing all the cancer). Steve later told me he was sitting there next to me, feeling awkward, not being able to answer the question. He said Kusum was standing behind me, not wanting me to see her because she was still crying since getting the phone call with the news an hour after my surgery started. I asked Steve if the clock was wrong. I didn't understand how it was that early, how the surgery was finished so quickly. I remember my surgeon coming in the room, telling me they didn't go through with the procedure as he discovered more cancer when doing the preliminary look inside. Too much disease to justify the surgery. I must have fallen back asleep because I don't remember much after that.

I spent the next 4 days recovering from the surgery. The first couple of days were the worst, especially after they removed the epidural. Yet I was able to begin walking, which helps the healing. Bowels go to sleep and gas gets trapped and that pain exacerbates the pain from the incisions and subsequent swelling. The day I was leaving the hospital, I finally asked for an enema because the pain meds weren't touching the pain from the intestinal back up. The nurse worked magic with a technique I'm surprised they don't use with every patient recovering from abdominal surgery...the Harris Flush. You can look it up if you're interested. I asked the surgeons days earlier why no one invented a catheter for gas because that would relieve the pain so many experience. This method did just that and I'll be forever grateful!!

When I left the hospital, it hit me. Wham...the endless tears, the sadness, the reality that the cancer had spread to new places in the 6 weeks since the surgeon looked inside and said I was a great candidate for this surgery. I am still left with so many questions. From what I understood, the biology of the cancer I have is very aggressive, so even if he'd done the surgery earlier, I most likely would have had a recurrence quickly. I see my surgeon next week and have my list of questions. I meet with my oncologist the following day. I hope we'll work on a plan that will help put the brakes on this spread of disease and even see it disappear. I've been a little in denial of where I'm at right now. I enjoyed 5 glorious weeks without getting chemotherapy....5 weeks where I could eat what I wanted, 5 weeks of less fatigue, 5 weeks of no needles in my port, no chemo in my body, no stink of that chemo coming out my pores for days, not driving to San Francisco twice a week every other week. All this beautiful time feeling so good, but the disease was taking advantage of this time. What trade offs we face to fight disease.

My future is uncertain (who does not have an uncertain future) in many ways. Yet, when I was talking with a friend yesterday, something hit me. LOVE. LOVE...
I realized that one of the most important things to me has been the opening up to love. "....*I've learned you can get through the bad times and keep looking for better ones, as long as you have people who love you.*"
I have to say, I've found the better times. I am living the better times, because I have found LOVE. I feel love from every one of you! The kindness, the goodness, the generosity, the open hearted love. I have learned to accept love, to let it in. And, something that is very important to me is to love back. To let others know how much I love them. I hope you know how much you all mean to me and the love I have for you. It may sound corny to hear it, but I truly feel so much love. I may not be good at writing back, returning texts or phone calls, but I feel love and appreciation towards you.

I remember several years ago I had been thinking a lot about death. I'd been reading about it and would talk with my friends about it. I would ask if people thought it better to die quickly, as with a heart attack, or slowly, knowing you're dying, as with cancer or some other terminal illness. There were pros and cons to each. But one thing I thought about was being able to let people know how much they mean to you and how much you love them. Since we never know how we're going to die, I thought it would be good to start living as if each day were the last, and try to let my friends and family know how much they mean to me, how much I love them. Of course, I'm not perfect and not always expressive, but I try to communicate my love.

So, thank you for your love. Thank you for the incredible support. Thank you for letting me share my thoughts, of walking with me through all the scary places and thank you for sharing your life with me.

I better stop because I've probably repeated myself 100 times and I should get to bed before the sun rises.

Big, big hugs,
leslye/Mukti

November 4, 2021

I was feeling...very deflated, very sad, very disappointed and very scared about what the progression of the cancer all would mean for me. I was focused on the body healing at first. Once discharged from the hospital, the news really hit me. I go in and out of sadness around this. I met with the surgeon on Tuesday and he explained why he made the choice he made. He said the fact that it grew in the 5 weeks meant the biology of the cancer would not have been favorable for such a big surgery. It's better that I begin chemotherapy.

I have been healing from the surgery pretty well. I stopped the pain meds almost a week ago. I've been feeling a little under the weather the past few days...like I have a low grade fever. That sucks because I was feeling really good before that. Saturday I took a 2 hour walk...but then slept for a few hours. I've been able to hike up hills as well. So feeling like I've got a low grade fever now bums me out. We'll start heading back home this weekend.

I will start chemotherapy the first week of December. Yuck! I'm a little worried about the cancer in the ovary. I don't know if it's a new primary or a metastasis. I asked the surgeon if it was IN the ovary or ON and he couldn't really answer.

I'm going to try to really enjoy the month of November since I won't be on chemo. Just want my belly to heal up...it always hurts, but just not enough to take pain meds.

November 11, 2021

Dear All,

I apologize for the belated update!
It's hard to know where to begin, or even how to begin. I'll just blurt this out.
The surgery didn't go as planned.
There, I said it.

As you all know, it was painstakingly difficult to make the decision to have Cytoreductive Surgery in the first place. However, based on my diagnostic laparoscopy in September, it felt like it was the best path to choose. It was an opportunity to get the cancer out of my body, at least for some time, if not for years!

We headed to San Diego feeling very supported and loved. We were introduced to our friends' family, who took good care of us as we arrived in San Diego. They offered so much care and were willing to be there as support after the surgery. My daughter arrived the night before surgery (it's such a blur to me right now) so she and Steve could accompany me to the hospital in the morning.

Once in the hospital pre-surgical room, where I had to once again wash my body with disinfectant, brush my teeth with disinfectant, and scrub out my nose with disinfectant, I took photos of it all and sent them to Steve and Kusum. I was going for some humor as q-tips were hanging out of my nostrils, my nose all yellow, my body tinted yellowish red. It wasn't the same as having them there, but we did get some laughs (I needed as many laughs as possible!!).

As the morning progressed, and they put an IV line in me (hitting the vein in such a way that the sheets had a good circle of bright red blood), a doctor came in to give me an epidural. I was very nervous about getting one, but I think they must have begun giving me something to calm my nerves as I don't remember much after getting that in my upper spine. It actually didn't hurt like I expected it to. I don't remember much of what happened after that. I think it's funny that my surgeon told me I asked for more drugs so that I was less conscious because I don't remember anything! I don't remember leaving the pre-surgery room or arriving into the operating room. I do, however, remember waking up in the recovery room.

It was kind of surreal there because, as out of it as I was, I remember seeing the clock on the wall above the door. It said 10:45. 10:45!!!! I had gone into surgery around 8:30, and it was 10:45. Steve was there and I asked him if the clock was broken. Then I began asking if they got all the cancer. I asked if I got the HIPEC (heated chemotherapy in the belly, which, BTW, we found out the day before surgery that it wasn't covered by insurance!) as well. I only remember the doctor sitting next to me, with concern in his eyes, saying, we didn't go on with the surgery. There was too much disease. I don't remember much after that.

I was in the hospital for 5 days, healing from the incision. All energy was focused on healing my body so I could go home, or rather, our temporary San Diego home. Some friends we'd recently met had offered us a place to stay...a family condo they had, right across the street from a state beach. I wanted to be there instead of the hospital. So I walked as much as possible, and weaned off IV pain meds to oral pain meds. I had to get my digestive system operating (hard to do while on pain meds).

Once "home" it hit me. They didn't get the cancer out. And I have more cancer all over my insides and it's on the uterus, the ovary, the pelvic floor. Wham! The depression hit. The fear of what to do now! I felt sad and angry and scared.

I'm so grateful we had a place to stay that was cozy and comfortable. We rented an electric recliner which I slept in the entire time which made it easier on my abdominal muscles. I got out and walked a little farther each day. The beach was only a couple of blocks away. It was healing to go to the ocean. I had my support group meetings on zoom and even met with one of the people from that group in person before we left San Diego.

So, what's the plan? I'm getting a CT scan to get a baseline so we can use it to measure if the chemo is working. Of course, all the scans missed the disease the surgeon saw and felt, except for the ovary, because that changed size. However, some of the disease is big enough to be seen on scans and I guess we'll use that to measure the success of the chemotherapy. I'll also be getting a monoclonal antibody, Avastin, after my incision is completely healed so there is no risk of bleeding. It's strange how a drug that is used as an antiangiogenic (which cuts off the blood supply to cancer cells) can also cause bleeding. Perhaps that is due to the fact that it can raise the blood pressure. I'm a little nervous to have a new drug added, but if it does the job without too many harmful side effects, I'm willing to try it.

I also have the support of an integrative care team, which I believe has kept my body strong throughout all this. I know I'm fortunate to have this amazing support.

I've also been getting so much support and education through an online group called COLONTOWN. I think because of the education and push for patient advocacy that COLONTOWN promotes, I'm still alive today. I've learned so much since my diagnosis (that had a 16 month prognosis), changed oncologists, gotten second and third opinions, etc. I'm learning, reluctantly, about this cancer, and am relentless when it comes to researching and asking my oncologist questions. My poor oncologist!

Thank you all for your love and support. You helped make it possible to go to San Diego to attempt this healing. I will be consulting with a surgeon in Chicago in a couple of months because he's also an expert in peritoneal cancer. I will see if I'm a candidate for this surgery again. In the meantime, I'm hoping there will be some advances in more targeted treatments for peritoneal disease, or perhaps some advances in making immunotherapy work for more types of tumors. So we start again in December, making the trip up to San Francisco twice a week, every other week, for treatment. Time to kick a**.

With so much love and gratitude,
Leslye/Mukti

March 19, 2022

Hospice Theology

Me: Hey God.

God: Hey John.

Me: What should I say to somebody who is about to die?

God: The exact same things you should say to everybody else whenever you have a chance.

Me: What's that?

God: I love you.
      I love you so.
      I forgive you.
      I'm sorry.
      I'm blessed to know you.
      I'm so grateful to you.
      I think that you are beautiful.
      I can't wait to see you again.
      I love you.
      I love you so.

****

{we are roommates in hospice care together and
every conversation we share
could be the most important moment in our lives}

{you and I are both dying right now so let's not
leave a single word unspoken between us ~ let's
speak the softest poetry to each other by
moonlight
because one of us might not physically be here in
the morning}

{we are fading stars calling to each other across
the vast universe to bathe each other in the softest
light of love one last time

before we slip through the vortex and back into
time}

{together we can build a confessional out of the
gentle glances we give each other while we hold
hands
and quietly pardon every scar we carved into each
other before we knew any better}

{if we remember that every heartbeat is being
counted then there will never be any ordinary
seconds spent between us

*~ each breath we share will be draped in
importance}*

*{in this planet of 8 billion hospice patients there is
so much magic and so many chances to brush
each other with rose petals
before we are swept away by resurrection}*

*let's lace our hands
as if eternity is opening
up the veil into the great
mystery right in front of us*

*let's feel our fingers against
each other as if this is the
last time we will touch before
we become celestial kites*

*let's part our lips and say
what we should have said
to each other years ago*

*I love you.
        I love you so.
        I forgive you.
I'm sorry.
        I'm blessed to know you.
        I'm so grateful to you.
I think that you are beautiful.
        I can't wait to see you again.
        I love you.
I love you so.*

        ~ john roedel

I've been loving this poet and his poetry...a lot! I've
been sharing his poetry on facebook. I just can't
get enough. I love his poetry! All of it. He describes

grief, love, life so authentically and poignantly.

(Warning...I'm writing during my 48 hour chemo treatment, one day after the infusion that includes steroids. I'm a mixture of being out there in the ethers and being buzzed by steroids. Oh, let's not forget day 3 of fasting. So, forgive my lack of writing skills.)

Death and dying has been on my mind. It had been something I thought a lot about way before my diagnosis. Experiencing the loss of so many near and dear but not knowing how to deal with it, as well as never being able to talk about death as a child, despite the fact that my father died when I was 9 and my step dad died when I was 11, had made me very uncomfortable around death and people with terminal illnesses. I didn't know what to say, how to comfort, or how to move on with the feelings that were inside me. I began reading about death and dying. I read many Stephen Levine books, signed up for the One Year to Live workshop, joined numerous Death Cafe's, and even looked into what it takes to be a death doula. Reading about death showed me it was all about life.... being in the present, being my own authentic self, appreciating the moment.

However it was with my diagnosis of a scary rare form of colon cancer (have you gotten your colonoscopy???) that I really began to look at death. Suddenly the proximity of my death seemed closer than ever. I remember experiencing life, but not being part of it. Everywhere we went, I imagined life went on, and I was no longer part of it. I began to feel into that. A group of people sitting in the cafe sipping coffee and eating scones would still go on, but I would never be in that cafe again. People would still be bringing packages to the post office, but I'd never drop off my mail and chat with Julie again. I felt like a ghost. I was living but not living. It was a weird experiment. The vocabulary of death and dying and all that encompasses is becoming more familiar to me. You want to do something really weird? Imagine your lifeless body in a cardboard box, your family and friends leaving poetry or flowers in the box, covering your body with all these expressions of love. Then imagine that box being pushed into an inferno, the contents to be burnt to ash. It's a strange thing, but I've been doing that to get used to the reality of dying. Dying, something we're all going to do. As John Roedel says in his poem, "In this planet of 8 billion hospice patients..."

The other thing I started doing was working on the baggage I didn't want burdening me when I died. I had to learn about forgiveness. Self forgiveness was the hardest, and I'm still challenged by it. Regrets are painful arrows in the heart. So I tried to come to terms with all of that. I learned to open up to the love flowing towards me, trying to wrap my head and heart around feeling worthy of it. I also allowed myself to express my love to others without feeling embarrassed. Despite having a terminal illness, I was feeling braver to speak my truth, to love more fiercely, to feel tenderness, acceptance and a lot of love. Love is the theme I guess. Don't get me wrong...this is a work in progress. I'm still bitchy, grumpy, defensive and throw temper tantrums sometimes. I still have issues with self worth. I get angry and hurt if I feel criticized or unheard (not very NVC language, my NVC friends). Yet my heart has opened in ways I couldn't imagine. I wish I'd had the courage to live like this decades prior to this diagnosis. But, ah, lose the regrets!

I can't remember the last time I wrote an update on living with stage 4 cancer and the race that is going on inside my abdominal cavity. I know the world continues to present horrific realities to us, so much violence, pain and suffering. How do we go on when there is so much suffering around us? Uh oh, this brings up another poem (because it reminds me of a Buddhist practice we can do when we feel despair and the need to do something):

Send Love--It Matters
by Carrie Newcomer

Somewhere someone needs help.
Send love. It matters.
If you can't get there yourself,
Then take a deep breath.
Breathe in the weight of their troubles,
Breathe out and send all those burdens
into the Light
Where sorrows can be held
With the most tender and infinite grace.
Breathe in what you can do
Breathe out what you can't change.
Spool out a thread of connection.
Send courage and calm.
For the nights can be long
And filled with shadows
And sometimes terrible
Unexpected waters will rise
Somewhere someone needs help.
Send love.
It matters.

Back to the update (and I apologize for my rambling).

As you all know, I had an aborted surgery. This was a surgery that could have removed all the cancer from my abdominal cavity. I was so scared of such an intense surgery, but had decided it was a shot at removing cancer and possibly being free of it for quite some time. But too much cancer had grown during the time I was off chemo to prepare for the surgery. The cancer had spread after the aborted surgery too as I couldn't resume chemotherapy for a couple of months while my incision healed. I thought, oh shit, I missed the boat, I've reached the point of no return. Yet we started chemo. After the first treatment, I experienced a bowel obstruction. It started with feeling nausea after eating a bowl of soup. I have never vomited with chemotherapy. I think fasting helps keep that in control. I just feel queasy and food tastes horrible, but thank goodness, I haven't had days of vomiting. That's why this scared me. I took some Ativan, since it's supposed to help with nausea. Minutes after I took it, I began projectile vomiting. My poor Steve...standing and watching as I heaved the contents of my belly. Steve, the guy who gags when seeing others barf, or having to pick up dog shit, or deal with other bodily fluids. I don't know how he did it, but there he was, cleaning the bathroom that was hit with my fire extinguisher speed orange vomit that not only went into the toilet, but on the toilet, the wall behind the toilet, the floor. This was repeated again and again until there were only dry heaves left. I don't know if there is a God somewhere that brings two people together, but I'm forever grateful that whatever it is, we found each other. This man is the BEST caregiver in the world. He takes me to all my treatments despite my complaints about how he drives (we go to UCSF), He has sat with me during treatment, shoveling ice into my mouth when I had a chemo that created cold sensitivity.

He changed the ice packs on my hands and feet for 2 hours. He's slept on couches in the hospitals after my surgeries, and he cleans the contents of my stomach as they shoot like a fire hose all over the bathroom. And he still loves me!!! And I love him dearly. I can't sing his praises enough. I just feel like the luckiest person to have such a caring partner.

After 4 cycles of chemo, we saw some shrinkage and no new disease. I say this with cautious optimism because it's hard to see the extent of disease with this type of cancer. It's flat, mucinous, and more like 1000 grains of sand covering organs. However, seeing shrinkage gave me some hope!! No more obstructions, I could eat a little better and I was feeling good.

My family arrived from Bali the night after my vomit session. We had an amazing, wonderful, memory making visit. Singing and dancing talent shows, art/craft projects, hiking, cooking, laughing together. We decided to take a trip to Joshua Tree, somewhere we'd never been. It's all about creating memories, and we had an amazing time doing so. Soul medicine.

In the last month or so I began to experience that feeling of fullness in the upper abdomen. It was hard to eat a full meal. This feeling is familiar and I know what it means. We went to UCSF to see if it was ascites and to get it drained if it was. Turns out, once again, to be tumor invasion, not fluids. Cancer is so damn smart. It learns to work around the chemotherapy, becoming resistant to the drugs. I do an integrative approach to treatment, having a robust herbal supplement to both keep my body strong with treatment and to try to stop the growth of cancer. Yet, this is what happens when you're on chemo for life. It eventually stops working, and we have to find other treatments that might work. I tell my killer T cells to see the cancer growth, these selfish rogue cells that think they need to consume the available space inside my abdominal cavity, and munch away. I visualize the cancer being very visible to these cells so they don't miss it. Maybe you can visualize that too if it resonates with you.

Yesterday I began a monoclonal antibody infusion along with my regular chemo. The drug wasn't offered at first because it works better with left sided tumors and mine was a right sided tumor. Yet in second line treatment, it can work. We'll see in 2 months when I get scans. I'll have a scan next week to get a baseline. I'm getting prepared for the dermatitis this drug causes. The range is amazing...from full body rash to only face, head, chest and back. There are other weird side effects, like hair growth in unusual places, including long eyelashes. Who doesn't like long eyelashes? But these get annoyingly long and irritating to the eyes. It's funny because the only thing that's been going on with my hair is exodus from my body. I have very few eyelashes, very thin eyebrows, bald spots on my head, and, while I never shaved my underarms anyway, now I wouldn't have to.

Having cancer is humbling. It forces one to do things they may not have done before. I never took drugs unless I was deathly ill with an infection. I avoided x-rays as much as possible. My family went through those x-ray machines at the airport but I always asked for the pat down. This created anxiety for my poor family as it seemed they punished those of us who wanted pat downs by making us wait a long time...making you think you're going to miss your plane. Now my body is a drug filtering machine and I've stopped studying the myriad of side effects. I also get more CT scans ever...every 2 months!!! Perhaps it's the reality that cancer will kill me faster than any secondary cancer from all the radiation and poison that allows me to surrender. Or maybe these things promise me a few more years. Who knows. I stopped trying to figure it out. Surrender...a good word.

In my quest for answers, because I'm a research junkie and am looking for options all the time, I found an amazing surgeon. He is committed to seeing people with my kind of cancer survive. His passion is palpable. He saw things on my pathology reports that didn't look right to him. The histology of my tumors left questions about where the primary cancer really was. Though the mass was in my small and large intestine, the markers pointed to an upper gastric primary. He had all my slides sent to his hospital so his top pathologist could look at them again. He has brought my case to the tumor board twice. Now he is requiring more testing of the tumor tissue to see if there are answers. Was my primary in the colon, the appendix (which is really where he thinks it originated) or in the upper gastric area...pancreas, etc...? Finding the answer will inform what treatment will be best for me. I may be eligible for another surgery. I'll know in a couple of months and will write an update. He gave us hope.

I mentioned I get my CT scan next week. This will be after 8 treatments. I'm not optimistic that it will show shrinkage because of the way I've been feeling. However, I'm getting braver with receiving bad news. I've learned that means look harder for solutions. I'm fortunate to have great doctors helping me. My palliative care team helps keep me as pain free as possible. I've got a swarm of loving and supportive friends. I've got the most amazing family one could hope for. I can't express the gratitude I have. It brings happy tears to my eyes as I sit here writing this. I'm so grateful for your love and support, riding along on this journey with me, offering prayers, good vibes, music, art projects, flowers, food, visits, hikes, comfortable furniture for me to recover in, and so much more. The love...the incredible love, love, love.

Thank you so much!! I love you all. I'm blessed to know you, I think that you're beautiful and I'm so grateful to have you in my life. You have truly graced my life with your presence. I love you.

xoxoxo
Mukti/leslye

April 3, 2022

I've started a new treatment that is supposed to shrink tumors. It's quite painful on the rest of my body. It creates a horrible rash that is hot and painful. I imagine this is what a chemical peel must feel like...except I won't get the benefit of that We'll see in May if the tumors have shrunk. The cancer in my ovaries is growing. I'm alarmed at how the blood markers rise every two weeks. I'm not sure what I'll do. On the one hand I want them removed from my body. But surgery means off treatment for awhile and, well, it's another surgery. It's a shitty situation. There is no cure so it's poison my body to try to keep tumors from killing me... until they become drug resistant.
I get where this is all leading, so it's a matter of living the best I can with the time given to me. And praying for a peaceful, joyous death.

If tumors behave, I really want to try to go to Bali in the summer. If that's not possible, I want a road trip!

May 12, 2022

Living and dying with stage 4 cancer, the dying part has been on my mind lately. This is mostly due to complications I've been having recently.

"We need not die defeated by death, feeling a failure, disappointed, constipated with remorse. It is possible to die at peace, mostly without pain, still learning, filled with gratitude." ~Stephen Levine from A Year to Live

The above may be true, yet it's hard to ignore that death can also be quite a messy thing. Who really knows what goes on behind those closed eyes, that mostly vacant body? I'm walking the path of faith, trust, open to love, scared of pain, wondering what the future looks like, wondering how death might feel, and what will happen in the great beyond.

I've been feeling angry lately. Not because I have cancer. Not because it's progressing. Not because I'm dying. I'm not the person who said, "why me?" when I was diagnosed. Yes, I've gotten angry at times these past 2.5 years. I've gotten angry when I was scared I was going to die without seeing my son and family that lives in Indonesia. Covid made that fear a big reality but my son made sure to get himself and his family back to California to see me. He's been here twice now (and stayed 2-3 months each time) since covid and cancer. He made my dreams come true!

I've gotten angry that my daughter, a nurse, who had to work without proper PPE during covid (pre-vaccine) sat in my backyard for 10 months instead of in my house. Some of her patients had covid and because I was on chemo, she was worried about possibly giving it to me. I longed to hug her, to watch movies with her, to have her sit in my house and eat with us. My heart broke for that year and I'm not sure it has ever really repaired itself. Fuck covid and fuck cancer (sorry for my language...just feeling this way lately).

We added a new drug to my chemo in mid March. By the second infusion, I developed the worst skin toxicity response. I've never felt that bad, not even when the tumor was blocking my intestine. I spent 3 weeks on a couch or in bed, cold towels on my red blistered face. Oxycodone was needed so I could get some relief from the 100's of blisters that covered my lips, cheek, tongue, throat, face, chest and back. This was not quality of life!! I got chills and a slight fever. Because my oncology team was worried I was getting an infection, I was put on antibiotics. Never did it cross our minds that I might have covid. Covid! If any of you are close to me, you know I'm one of the most cautious (paranoid??) people around others. I always wear a mask...a KN95 or N95, even when I go to the farmer's market! Where I picked up covid, with a mask on, is beyond me. Could it have been the unmasked and coughing people when I went to Trader Joe's? Could it have been the infusion center, where some patients take their masks off to eat and drink during their chemo? I don't know. Anyway, I tested positive for covid and while that disease passed through me without problems, the consequences I suffered were cancer progression. This is why my family was so careful about protecting me. Covid may be a slight cold, a sniffle, a headache, fatigue. Nothing to worry about for most people. For people on active cancer treatment, it's almost a death sentence if you have very aggressive cancer. I was denied treatment for 5 weeks. Yup, 5 weeks of no poison to stop my very aggressive tumors from taking over my body. And that is what they did. Suddenly there was no room for the fluid that develops from peritoneal disease to leave my body. Between the tumor burden (the tumors are on my liver, diaphragm, omentum, ovaries, small bowel surface, pelvis, ovaries, uterus...basically on every organ in my abdomen) and the fluid, my life has been hell! I've had two paracentesis procedures in two weeks. I now have them scheduled weekly. If anyone is familiar with cancer, you know ascites like this is not a good sign!

I'm angry at UCSF and their covid policy. I'm angry they didn't have a patient advocate. I'm angry because I found out, by looking on their website and talking to the Epidemiology and Infectious Disease department that I should have been offered chemotherapy. They have isolation rooms for people with covid on time-sensitive treatment. I actually didn't have covid anymore, but their 20 day policy put my life in danger.

I'm angry that I received this letter from my oncologist:

Hello Leslye,
I heard that you spoke to G...... via a provider backline. I spoke with her also.
To clarify: your treatment does not qualify as lifesaving because there is not an expectation of cure. You will come off of isolation per Cancer Center policy on May 1. You are not permitted to

*receive treatment tomorrow. This does not impact
your overall prognosis.
If you want to discuss your concerns about this
policy further, you are welcome to contact Patient
Relations. We are committed to providing the same
high level of care to all patients.*

Was she implying that palliative treatment
disqualifies me from treatment that is helping
prolong my life? Was it okay, because I'm going to
die from this disease one day, to stop my
treatments, to not fight for my right for treatment,
because it's not going to save my life, so it's okay
to expedite my death? The lack of treatment HAS
impacted my overall prognosis. I went from
possibly having a year or so (according to the
NEW oncologist, she was optimistic about keeping
me around for a couple of years...before this
progression) to looking at 3-4 months if we can't
turn this around.

Hopefully my treatments will begin at Stanford
next week. I do not trust my UCSF oncologist
anymore...to have such disregard for my life
because I have stage 4 incurable cancer! Idid all
the research and found that I should have been
offered treatment and someone messed up and it
cost me precious time. I will be taking a new drug
that comes with a set of scary side effects, one of
them bowel perforations and profuse bleeding. It
stops blood vessels from forming, so hopefully
cancer will let go the grip on my organs and begin
to shrink away. I'll also have to go back on to the
very neurotoxic platinum drug, oxaliplatin. I'm
strong, so hopefully, my body will withstand these
very, very strong and toxic treatments. It's always
a balance to give enough poison to beat back the
cancer, but not enough to kill the host.

Today I get an MRI, and we'll hopefully see what's going on inside there. If we get stability with the majority of my tumors, I'll be able to get the ovaries removed. Ovaries are sanctuary organs, staying safely protected from chemotherapy, but not cancer. My ovaries are growing so we'll see if surgery will be on the table in the near future.

There is much uncertainty, but the thing that is certain is I know i'm loved and I know I love. I have received so much love and support from you all...and have struggled to get past the idea that I just don't deserve all this.

I know that when my time comes, your LOVE and support and hands and hearts will be right there with me...walking me to the next great adventure. While I don't know what it's like, I imagine I'll be there beside you all, always, and giving all the love and support right back. We are forever family, forever connected and I feel the immense love. Thank You!!!

(As I'm facing some scary treatments and tests, I'd appreciate the visualization that my body is protected from harmful and life-threatening side effects, while the cancer is not protected from that at all. And thank you for letting me express my anger, without judgement. Feelings come up and we are human and it's okay to experience the spectrum....)

As always, please let me know if you want to be removed from my email updates....no one should be receiving this if it's unwanted! I will NOT be offended. I am respectful of your needs and boundaries. I also don't have everyone's email address and if you know my friends and family who would like to know what's going on, please forward or give me the email address. T

Much, much, much love!
Leslye/Mukti

May 31, 2022

Dear Dr. ..... and Patient Relations,

I'm writing to express a grievance about how my covid positive case was handled. I'm especially upset because I had nothing but negative PCR covid tests 3 days after my positive one and even tested negative with an antigen test (the tests you recommend your staff to take so they can return to work within 5-7 days after being positive for covid) the same day I had a positive PCR test.

I feel the outcome of my life expectancy has been compromised with this decision as the cancer has progressed during this time and my quality of life has diminished due to the side effects that have occurred with increased tumor burden.

A little background:

On April 7th, I began to have a slight fever (99.5) and chills, along with 100's of blisters all over my face, mouth, lips, cheeks, tongue and throat. I was having a severe reaction to an EGFR inhibitor. I was instructed to begin taking antibiotics right away for fear of a possible infection.

My fever and chills resolved in a day but the pain I had from the drug continued. Because I was having an in person appointment on 4/11, and the e-check in asked about fever and chills, which I'd not had before, I decided to get a covid test, despite the fact that the symptoms were gone. I'm very conscientious about covid and not spreading it (which is why, unlike many patients in the infusion room who remove their masks to eat soup, drink tea, eat snacks, or simply pull it down because they don't like it, I keep my uncomfortable N-95 on the entire day, never even taking a sip of water).

I was surprised that my result was positive, but relieved that I lived through covid with barely a symptom (was the fever and chills covid, or was it the pending infection since it seemed the antibiotics took my slight fever away). I was also happy to see that 3 days after the positive test, all of my PCR tests were negative.

I was told I could not have treatment for 20 days, despite the fact that my PCR tests were negative. My last treatment before my covid positive test was 3/30/2022, so my next treatment was due 4/13. I diligently researched the covid policy posted on the UCSF website. (I've attached two documents below showing what I read.)

According to YOUR VERY OWN policy, I should have been able to receive treatment on 4/21, which would have been 10 days past my covid positive test. I wrote to my team numerous times and got no response that indicated anyone was investigating my individual case. I heard back that ALL cancer patients fall under the "Severely immunocompromised" category simply because they are on treatment. When I talked to the person in the HEIP department, she informed me of a different scenario. She told me, yes, there is an umbrella that all cancer patients fall under, but individual cases should be evaluated. I have a NORMAL WBC, which does not make me severely *immunocompromised. As Dr. A… receives my labs every two weeks, she could have relayed that information to the person she spoke with in the HEIP department.*

To quote what is written on YOUR OWN POLICY: "Guidelines are intended to assist with clinical decision-making but cannot replace personalized evaluation and management decisions based on individual patient factors."
*I repeat: **but cannot replace personalized evaluation and management decisions based on individual patient factors.***

The other posted information on that page says: "Covid-19 positivity should not delay time-sensitive care."
*I would like to repeat that: **Covid-19 positivity should not delay time-sensitive care***
Yet, I was denied this very time-sensitive treatment. Also, why was the fact that my PCR tests were now negative not factored into this decision (attached my test two days after my positive test below) ? You allow your staff to return to work with a negative antigen test in 7 days, 5 days if there is a staff shortage (I saw your policy online).

I assumed my team, especially my oncologist who saw me go through an aborted surgery due to aggressive progression of my disease while I was off chemo for 4 weeks, would have been concerned that my disease would progress if I was denied treatment for 5 weeks and would have been assertive in finding out the correct protocol and have advocated for my treatment.

I can only guess at why this didn't happen.

1) UCSF policy that prevents the oncologist and NP from seeing a patient in person, (I've seen Dr. ..... 3 times in person over 1.5 years, and the NP once for a thorough exam pre treatment. Once in **nineteen treatments!** (It was supposed to be twice, but traffic was so bad one day I got there late...driving from Santa Cruz, there could always be an unexpected accident that will create a backup). This may mean that the oncologist is less familiar with an individual case as it's a very impersonal relationship.

2) The following letter from Dr. ....., which seems to say that since I'm stage 4 and incurable, missing treatment doesn't change my overall prognosis (so very wrong, as progression of disease DOES change the overall prognosis, as well as quality of life).

"Hello Leslye,
I heard that you spoke to G..... via a provider backline. I spoke with her also.
To clarify: your treatment does not qualify as lifesaving because there is not an expectation of cure. You will come off of isolation per Cancer Center policy on May 1. You are not permitted to receive treatment tomorrow. This does not impact your overall prognosis.
If you want to discuss your concerns about this policy further, you are welcome to contact Patient Relations. We are committed to providing the same high level of care to all patients.

Kind Regards,
Dr. ....."

According to the above letter, I was denied treatment because it is not life-saving, no expectation of cure. Well, I experienced tremendous tumor growth (my ovaries doubled in size according to the MRI I recently had) and began having relentless ascites, which I had to go to the ED to have drained. (I had mild ascites before this but never enough to even remove from my belly) I now have been drained twice within 10 days due to the extreme pain I had every day it's full. Does this letter mean it wouldn't matter if the cancer progressed, since my treatment is not life saving? If so, what a horrible situation to create for the patient you're giving palliative treatment to and trying to help extend their life, with quality and minimal pain. I was shocked to see this letter from you, Dr._..........., and I said that in my response to it. I put my life in your hands, I trusted you. I thought I struck gold when you became my doctor.

I will be slowly leaving the oncology department of UCSF. I can no longer trust that my life and my treatments will be a priority. I am sad to lose the relationship I had with Dr. ...., who is so smart and seemed so compassionate.

I have a great appreciation for the nurses who cared for me. Nurses who told me I should be seen in person by my oncologist. Nurses who told me other doctors were seeing patients now. Nurses who gave me loving care while filling my body with cancer fighting poison. The nurses are so attentive and caring.

I'm sad about this entire experience. I'm sad to move on. I spent countless hours on the road (living 80 miles away from UCSF) to have treatment at what was supposed to be an amazing cancer center. As a patient at UCSF oncology, I felt like a jacket on a rack at a dry cleaner....being whipped around from procedure to procedure, without

*human contact, except from the caring nurses. I'm
disappointed to find out how one can be treated so
impersonally there and that an oncology team
would allow their patient, who is known to
have progression when off treatment, to suffer as I
have.*

*Attached are your covid policies....policies that
seem to conflict with the cancer center's policy. I
hope there is some resolution for this before
another person is put in my situation...denial of
needed treatment to prevent progression of a
dangerous cancer (that feels like it has shortened
my life expectancy,) has caused me to need
repeated paracentesis (and the risk of infection
from that) due to the progression and the pain this
causes , and has broken my trust in the quality of
care that one expects from such a supposedly
quality cancer center.*

*I wish to take these grievances further than UCSF
as I believe this was a grossly dangerous decision
and would like it to be investigated further. Who
would you suggest?*

*In summary, I am very saddened and disappointed
in the mistreatment of my individual case, the
trauma I've experienced with the rapid growth of
tumors and having to go to the ED to get relief
from the extreme pain, and feeling anger that my
team allowed this to happen "because my
treatment is not life-saving." This is not what I
expected from a cancer center who is supposed to
do everything they can to see that I have less
tumor burden, great palliative treatments and
quality of life while I'm still on this planet.*

*I would appreciate a written reply.
Leslye Lawrence*

June 17, 2022

Do you like this poem? I like the last 2 lines.

Don't prioritise your looks my friend, as they won't
last the journey.
Your sense of humour though, will only get better
with age.
Your intuition will grow and expand like a majestic
cloak of wisdom.
Your ability to choose your battles, will be fine-
tuned to perfection.
Your capacity for stillness, for living in the moment,
will blossom.
Your desire to live each and every moment will
transcend all other wants.
Your instinct for knowing what (and who) is worth
your time, will grow and flourish like ivy on a castle
wall.
Don't prioritise your looks my friend,
they will change forevermore, that pursuit is one of
much sadness and disappointment.
Prioritise the uniqueness that make you you,
and the invisible magnet that draws in other
like-minded souls to dance in your orbit.
These are the things which will only get better.
Donna Ashworth

July 22, 2022

Just a quick note because I've been horrible about
writing lately.

My heart has been pierced by love again and
again! Thank you for the incredible birthday gift! I
was bowled over by the videos, the emails, the
cards, the LOVE! I'm slow, but plan on sending
thank you cards. It could take months :-)

I realize you see someone in me that I'm not familiar with. I suppose struggling most of my life with feelings of fear, self-loathing, lack of self-worth, it's hard to see the person you see in me. I struggle with feeling like an imposter. I want you to know I am sometimes mean, I am grumpy, I am scared, I struggle with being organized, I procrastinate, I'm unproductive, I get angry, and on and on and on.

I am beginning to heal the fear, and those feelings of self hatred that has kept me away from the people I value and love so much, but it is a process. Thank you for helping me believe in myself, for helping me find strength and courage. Mostly, thank you for being by my side with so much love, allowing me to love you deeply...to open up to the most vulnerable, raw place and let the balm of love come in and out. I haven't known devotion or faith or commitment in my life, though I have strived for it. However, these past few years my heart has opened and LOVE has really meant something. I truly feel it. I didn't seek it and was surprised by the strong sense of LOVE. People use that word all the time, almost reflexively, and I've been guilty of that too. Yet, it is different, even as I struggle to feel a sense of belonging. I do feel love...love from all of you whom I have shielded myself against. I can't express the gratitude I feel, but if it means anything, I know when I die, I will die feeling full and complete with LOVE (well, I really have no idea how I'll feel..scared? content? peaceful? angry?). (Oh my, I'm one of those people who uses too many parentheses....and these darn ellipsis...there must be a name for that besides poor style).

I didn't expect to see my 63rd birthday. Ever since I was diagnosed with this horrid disease, I've been learning to live with facing mortality. While I dive deeply into dying, trying to understand and learn as much about it as possible, trying to resolve past regrets and feel a sense of peace and contentment, I am also fully living. Something about knowing the Sword of Damocles is hanging over my head has allowed a deeper appreciation of everything, even acceptance of my shortcomings and lack of achievements.

I'm on chemotherapy for life, which means I get these strong chemicals which knock me out for a week every two weeks, for the rest of my life, or until it stops working. We also try to keep my body strong by using the medicine of the plants. My healing also comes from my community. The LOVE I receive is medicine, the prayers are medicine. My spiritual life is medicine. My friends are medicine. Meditation and movement is my medicine. My family is my medicine. The incredible doctors who truly care for me as a person and do everything they can to help me is my medicine (it's not the only chemicals they pump into me, it's the love and desire for me to live the best life, the care of ME that is the medicine). It is all healing for me. Please note the difference between cure and healing. Dying from cancer is not a failure. Cancer is a disease that grows uncontrollably. There is only so much all these modalities of healing can help. I loathe when people say "They lost their battle" because no, they didn't. Living and loving is a gift. Everyone dies. We don't lose our battle because we die. We have a disease like anyone else does. Something about cancer makes people think that the person who got cancer just isn't good enough, doesn't pray enough, isn't positive enough, doesn't eat healthy, etc, etc, etc. That's just not true.

We're preparing to leave for a week. I never thought I'd see Shasta again or the Oregon coast. Yet here we go....off to some beautiful places that mean a lot to me. I'm grateful. When we return, I'll have my 38th or 39th treatment (now I'm losing count). I'll be consulting with the surgeon about removing my ovaries. I'll be meeting the amazing scientist oncologist in LA about clinical trials. There will be many decisions ahead....the road will have many roads from which to choose. All will have possible benefits or consequences. This is life with cancer...in a word...UNCERTAINTY. So one must make a decision (I'm the worst at making decisions) and move forward with faith and acceptance.
Much, Much, Much LOVE
leslye/Mukti

September 23, 2022

*I am filled with quiet
joy for no reason save
the fact that I'm alive.
The message I receive
is clear -- there's no time
to lose from loving, no
place but here to offer
kindness, no day but this
to be my true, unfettered
self and pass the flame
from heart to heart.
This is the only moment that
exists -- so simple, so
exquisite, and so real.*

-Danna Faulds

These last few weeks have been hard. Several people who I cut teeth with in cancerland have passed on. These are people who lived life to the fullest. A few of them had exactly the same, aggressive cancer I have and it had metastasized to the peritoneum. Some had the same surgeon I had. Most were younger than me...athletic, positive, spiritual, fun loving, people with children under 18. It takes a piece of my heart every time I lose a friend. How can these people be my friends if I've never met them in person? We share a terminal disease, the complications, the fears, the hopes, the pain, the bad feelings from chemo, the recoveries from surgeries, support, education, love...so much love.

Then there are the handful of us who got bad news....cancer is spreading despite the surgeries, the chemotherapy, the clinical trials. Some have reached the end of the road for treatment and are transitioning to hospice. Some have had over 100 chemotherapy treatments and still live life to the fullest...working in a restaurant, riding a jetski for miles and miles every day, walks on the beach, camping, hiking, etc, as their bodies allow. Still the cancer grows.

I'm one of those that got bad news.

When Steve and I took our trip to Oregon in August, I remember waking up at Crater Lake with the thought: I want to live!! I want to live! I'm in pain, but I want to live. Don't get me wrong...I'm very aware I have a life-limiting disease that is aggressive and I've looked at death, and continue to do so, from every angle. I watch my son take the laundry to the laundry room and I think, one day I'm not going to be sitting here watching this. I imagine myself in the cardboard box, people offering flowers, notes, or whatever they want before my body is pushed into the incinerator. I see my family playing board games, my photo on the table smiling at them. I try to feel what death is, but I won't know until it happens. I do pray for a painless death, in as much as I can be provided with one. But that morning, in our van at Crater Lake, I thought...enough focusing on death, I'm focusing on living!

We had a great time, visiting long time friends, visiting beautiful places, camping, laughing, cooking with friends, etc. It was like life before cancer and covid. Oh, how joyful it was!!! (some photos below)

When we returned home, I had appointments with the brilliant doctors down in LA. We drove from one heat wave to another. I finally met Dr. Lenz in person. Oh what a brilliant scientist he is. Unfortunately for me, there are only a few options...and they are not new, innovative, sexy (his words) clinical trials. They are standard of care drugs that we hope will help me eke out a few more months. Idid get a big bear hug from him and we left feeling hopeful just being in his radar of care. I also went to the 'Disneyland' of cancer, City of Hope. I met with a mastermind of clinical trials. We were fortunate he came in to meet us on a day he isn't in the clinic. I was met with disappointing news there too. My cancer is aggressive, there is not much for people with signet ring cell cancer or peritoneal disease, I may get a few months more if I start taking oxaliplatin, but can also get permanent neuropathy and will have to stop using it at some point.

Well, we came home, ready to meet with my local oncologist and discuss treatment options. Luckily,

I do have a brilliant herbalist who looks at all my blood work and offers evidence based plant medicines to help my body be strong. And it's working because, despite the fact that the cancer is growing, I've never been neutropenic and my liver enzymes are always within range. In fact, most people will say I look so good they wouldn't know I have cancer (except I'm bald and I look 8 months pregnant due to the malignant ascites). I began the oxaliplatin, but at a very low dose....40%. The next treatment I moved it up to 50%. I was going to move it up to 60% on my next treatment, but that treatment never came. I began experiencing so much pain in my abdominal area. Ascites is causing complications.

For those who don't know, malignant ascites is a fluid that accumulates in the abdominal cavity. It comes from the tumors in the abdominal cavity in advanced cancers. I get a paracentesis regularly to drain the fluid, but the pockets of fluid are loculated, so they can only find one or two pockets and drain off some fluid, usually only one or two liters. However, that provides a little relief for a short time. The feeling I have is when you eat too much and need to unbutton your pants. Only I can't unbutton anything. I get shortness of breath and have constant pain. I've had to resort to pain meds when it gets really bad. The pain has been increasing and I ended up at the ER on 9/11 to find out why it hurts so badly. The CT scan showed the cancer has progressed...a lot. My left ovary is now 16 cm....up from 9 in July. I may have some cancer in the liver now. I had cancer ON the liver (and diaphragm, spleen, small bowel, ovaries, omentum, right pelvic area, uterus, and more) but never IN the liver. This means it's going systemic....something it hasn't done for 3 years. Today I returned from my 4th visit to the emergency department since Sept. 11. Nothing was done except reassurance that I don't have an infection in my ascites fluid. That is good because infection=sepsis=quick death. I will be having a drain put in my abdomen so I can drain the fluid when it gets too painful.

The other disappointing news I received was the cancer is now in my uterus. I'd begun having some vaginal bleeding a month or so ago. I had an endometrial biopsy to rule out a new cancer. What the pathology showed is that I've got cancer cells in the lining of my uterus and they have the same pathology as the colon cancer. This cancer is a very hungry and greedy monster. While I feed it poison, while I surround myself with love, while I have the best support system in the world, while I try to exercise and eat right (hard to eat when stomach is squished to the maximum), the cancer seems to like my body. It is invading new places. I guess I am attractive after all :-)

To top it all off, I tested positive for Covid last week. What a bitch Covid is!!! My cancer center wanted me to get a monoclonal antibody infusion (bebtelovimab) for Covid so I wouldn't get such a bad case. I debated because I don't like experimental drugs in my body, but I also didn't want to miss too much chemotherapy (as you all know I progressed tremendously last time I was denied treatment for 4.5 weeks). I got the infusion the second day as I was feeling worse and wanted to heal faster. I don't know if the antibody did it, but I got so freakin' sick. My fever was 104, my throat felt like anything I swallowed was transformed into knives, my headache didn't go away even with Tylenol. Ugh...it was no fun. I still get fevers from time to time. The ER doctor told me we don't know what to expect with covid, especially when people take the antibody, as they don't know enough about it. That makes me regret taking it. The sheet they gave me after the infusion said this antibody may interfere with my body being able to fight off future covid infections and may render vaccines ineffective. Damn!!!! It MAY? Well, I hope I don't get infected again. Steve just tested positive. That completes the cycle...now everyone who lives in my house has had covid. I expect to have a little more freedom for a couple of months...visiting friends, maybe going to hear live music, etc. We've been so scared of catching covid, so when we recover, we'll be able to see people without fear. Finally, visits with our family members!!!! Yay!! It's been so isolating trying to avoid covid. Many friends have stopped inviting us on hikes or visits or gatherings. While I understand, it hurts a little because I like to feel included even if we have to say no. We've had to be so careful, and now the worst has happened. I am too sick to get chemo so my cancer is probably growing. I'm going to have chemo and an MRI on Monday, so please keep good thoughts out for me. I'm a little worried about chemo while still fighting covid.

It's been an emotional roller coaster. The palliative care doctor I met with earlier this week (she's new and doesn't know me) was so concerned about my pain and the growth, she asked me if I've considered stopping treatment. She told me if I want quality time with my family in Indonesia, tell them to come sooner than November. I was heartbroken after that appointment. I had to talk to my kids and let them know the grim news. I was pleasantly surprised at how well taken the conversations were. I'm so proud of my children. They have had to put up with the reality of losing their mom. We've been lucky that I've outlived my prognosis, but we all know eventually my time will be up. I tell them how lucky I feel, how life is rich with love and connection and how blessed I am that I have this incredible family. This includes my Tara and her boys...I'm lucky to have bonus children and grandchildren...who have been there for me since the beginning, sacrificing as much as my children do. I am blessed to have the best partner in the entire world. He has devoted his life to being by my side, never abandoning me. He does it joyfully with a big yes, not out of duty. One of his big expressions of love is action, and boy does he take action. Steve, I love you with all my heart and can't believe how blessed I am to have been paired with you. We have had a great 21 years of adventure, growth, laughter, tears, and so much more.

I am blessed with a community who loves me and lets me know. You have opened up your arms and hearts to me in such a profound way. I never accepted love....I felt I was unworthy of love. You have shown me differently. Oh how I hope you know how much I love and appreciate you! I feel guilty because I don't always answer emails, can't always talk, haven't finished writing my thank you cards for the amazing birthday gift you gave me, etc. Please know I appreciate every ounce of love. You have brought us nourishing food, music, places to stay, you've kept in touch with texts, cards, you've dropped beautiful flowers and chocolate, veggies from your gardens, and so much more. If I've failed to thank you, I apologize!!! It means the world to me. I've said it before and I'll say it again, I will leave this world filled with so much love because of all of you. I have peace (most of the time), and I can truly say I am happy.

I'll close this with a beautiful quote from Stuart Scott, a sports broadcaster that died from appendiceal cancer in 2015, that describes how I feel about living and dying with cancer:

*When you die, it does not mean
that you lose to cancer.
You beat cancer by how you live,
why you live, and the manner
in which you live.
So live. Live. Fight like hell
and when you get too tired to fight,
lay down and rest
and let somebody else fight for you.*
Stuart Scott

In unending love,
leslye/Mukti

October 9, 2022

blessing the boats
by Lucille Clifton

*may the tide
that is entering even now
the lip of our understanding
carry you out
beyond the face of fear
may you kiss
the wind then turn from it
certain that it will
love your back   may you
open your eyes to water
water waving forever
and may you in your innocence
sail through this to that*

Oh, how does one deal with all the pain and suffering in this world? How do we read about another mass shooting of young children (in Thailand) and then go on with life? How do we witness the horrors of climate change and still go about our business? There is so much hatred and intolerance in the world....ever since I can remember as a young child. How do we survive? What gives our minds and hearts flexibility to live without falling into a permanent deep depression? Perhaps it is these things we witness that make us want to be better people. It's not easy...I've had a lifetime of being bitchy, mean, harmful, etc. mixed in with trying to be loving. But as I've aged, the way I try to deal with what goes on in this world is to try my hardest to be kind, to build bridges. Anger used to rule my actions. Now, I try to let love and compassion be the leading force. It's not always easy, but I think maybe this is how we, as individuals, who may feel helpless witnessing the world, deal with this. We plant seeds of love, kindness and caring. Whether it's getting politically involved, or talking to people who hold polar opposites of our beliefs with the goal of meeting as human beings rather than trying to prove our views as the only right view, whether it's doing random acts of kindness to friends and strangers....I don't know, but I think this is how I try to deal with the atrocities around me.

Personally, Steve and I have been going through this roller coaster. I had a very bad few weeks. I didn't get the easy version of Covid....I got the worst of it. Although my new cancer center had isolation rooms where I could have gotten my chemotherapy treatments, I was sent home, too sick to get chemo while fighting covid. It would have been a lethal combination. With lack of treatment, these tumors that love the inside of my belly took advantage and grew. With that growth, the malignant ascites was being produced faster than ever. I couldn't breathe, I couldn't eat, I could hardly drink as everything that tried to fit in my stomach hurt tremendously. My leg hurt so badly, and I discovered that I developed a blood clot. My family from Bali is arriving today. Last weekend, I didn't think I'd be alive to greet them. I was preparing to die.

Tuesday I went to UCSF and had 4 liters drained from my belly. 4 liters!! 9 pounds of fluid. The NP who did my paracentesis was surprised we got so much, by far the most I ever was able to have drained.The week before I'd only gotten 700cc out. Suddenly I felt alive again. I could breathe, I could walk, and we went and I had a plate of veggies and rice! Life came back into my body. Today is Sunday, and I'm going to see my family as soon as they arrive in Santa Cruz. I'm not bedridden, I'm out and about, despite still having about 4-6 liters of fluid that can't come out.

This is the roller coaster of terminal cancer. This is why every day is a gift. I've been fortunate to outlive the 1.5 year prognosis, but I have no idea how much longer I have. I'm malnourished, weaker than I've ever been, still have shortness of breath, etc. But I'm alive. And I'm making an effort to see as many of my beloved friends as possible.

Which brings me to the point of this email....We've decided to have a good-bye party/celebration of life/living funeral/opportunity for me to express gratitude/ whatever we're going to call it. (This from a person who has shied away from 63 years of birthday parties!!) In our death phobic society, having a good-bye party may seem weird. For me, living with the reality that my life is limited (as all our lives are...but a terminal illness brings that reality closer), we're going to celebrate life and death. I want to have this celebration when I am feeling good enough to appreciate gathering with everyone, knowing that my lifetime is limited.

So, please, if you can, keep November 6th open. Yes, it's a tentative date, as who knows what will happen between now and then. But we're going to plan on having some fun together, outside in a beautiful redwood grove. More details to come as we develop them. This is just a save-the-date so you can put it on your calendar.

With so much love and gratitude for all of you!
Leslye

October 19, 2022

It's been a crazy couple of months...I got really sick with Covid for 2 weeks, the cancer progressed, we were in the ER 5 times in 3 weeks, and many doctor visits weekly.
I'm at a place where tough decisions have to be made.
1) surgery to remove ovaries and uterus, but unknown if I'll recover from that due to all the other tumors growing while off chemo for recovery.
2) trying other chemo therapies that might be more effective because it seems this isn't working and it makes me very, very sick.
3) hospice
All the treatments are just to try to give me quality of life, not curative.
The main problem that affects my life now is the fluid that build in my belly. Two weeks ago, they got nine pounds of fluid out.
We're on our way to the hospital to get my belly drained again...it's a weekly thing now.

Anyway, I just wanted to say hello and tell you how much I love you.

AWAKENING NOW
by Danna Faulds

Why wait for your awakening?
The moment your eyes are open, seize the day.
Would you hold back when the Beloved beckons?
Would you deliver your litany of sins like a child's collection of sea shells, prized and labeled?
"No, I can't step across the threshold," you say, eyes downcast.
"I'm not worthy" I'm afraid, and my motives aren't pure.
I'm not perfect, and surely I haven't practiced nearly enough.
My meditation isn't deep, and my prayers are sometimes insincere.
I still chew my fingernails, and the refrigerator isn't clean.
Do you value your reasons for staying small more than the light shining through the open door?
Forgive yourself.
Forgive yourself.
Now is the only time you have to be whole.
Now is the sole moment that exists to live in the light of your true Self.Perfection is not a prerequisite for anything but pain.
Please, oh please, don't continue to believe in your stories of separation and failure.
This is the day of your awakening.

October 23, 2022 -
Leslye's "GOING AWAY PARTY"

October 24, 2022

Thank you for being with us at the beautiful, love-filled celebration.
Although I didn't have an opportunity to spend time with everyone, your presence was deeply felt. I'm trying to get things in order now as I have no idea when my final day is on this earth, in this body. Cancer is a disease of uncertainty so I am living each day, doing the best I can, in this very limited and increasingly painful body. And each day is a joy…I am blessed with so much love, a family that I get to see even if I can't get out much with them, friends who give so much love…so I'll take each day given to me in gratitude.

October 28, 2022

I've been diving in to death lately. For some reason (maybe the higher dose of Oxycodone I took because the pain is big) my mind keeps returning to that last moment, that last breath. Thoughts of being fully aware of it being my last breath are strong. Then I feel a bit of fear. Being aware of the final breath, of knowing the body will separate from the spirit…it's hard not to be a little frightened. Questions, questions, so many questions…will it be peaceful? This transition, this goodbye, this final breath as this body in this lifetime…oh, the finality of it. I try to imagine my guru Baba Hari Dass, my mom, the special people in my life who have passed before me…will my hand be lovingly held, will I be able to muster that goodbye, knowing my eyes will never again rest on my family…never again laugh and cry with them… never feel the various shapes of my loves in my arms. This is the hard part. May I truly let go.

I suppose the work/play of every day will be practicing this…giving and receiving the immense love…the tremendous, gigantic, omnipresent beautifully, brilliantly, bubbling-over ocean of love. How to live it and let go of it? Slipping out of the confines of this body, saying goodbye and knowing it's all going to be okay. My love will be with them forever. May their hearts be so full of my love now that it will be palpable to them forever.

I'm afraid I'm focusing on the dying process way more than researching the next treatment option. I've grown tired of that. I don't want to read about another clinical trial or another possible treatment. In fact, I'm finding myself repulsed by it all now.

It's been a lesson, observing how quickly things change in the body. Looking through pictures that aren't quite that old, I realized I can't do what I used to do even two months ago. I cried and thought, as I was laying in bed, legs elevated due to extreme edema, I have no quality of life anymore. I miss hiking, I miss walking on the beach, I miss camping. Suddenly a light went off and I was eased into peace. I DO have quality of life. It's a different life, one in which I can't use the body like I used to, but I'm surrounded by my people, my family, my community. This is GOLD! I have the best life ever. Yes, there is pain, yes I have a million loose ends to tie up, but I have my family and community of friends and there is so much love here, it's spilling over. Omg, to think I said I have no quality of life. I have the biggest QUALITY of LIFE ever.

I have an incredible family that has been engaging in talks of death and dying with me. They've had a new opportunity to try it on, get a little more familiar with the fact that I will not be here much longer. My granddaughter asks about all sorts of things that can possibly burn with me once my body is in the cardboard box, ready to be burned to ashes...can she paint a pumpkin and put it in the box with me? Will the beads that people held at the end of life ceremony be able to burn with me. Oh, the tears that fill my eyes as I write this, my chest heaving with sadness. How can I embrace the sadness and the love that is so big in my life?

Questions, questions...I'm only filled with questions...no answers.
I live each day, grateful to have one more day with all of you. This disease of uncertainty gives no clues as to when the end will come. The complications with my body are increasing, but I just don't know when I'll take my final breath.

You have made my life feel like it had purpose when I spent all my time searching for purpose. You have given me open hearted love, more than I could ever have imagined. You have made me feel valued as a person...something I lacked. You have helped me see that I am a good person, when all I felt was how bad a person I was. I feel so blessed. I don't know how I'm writing because my eyes are blurred with tears.

Thank you seems so inadequate to express what I feel...like a grain of sand in the big ocean....but that is what I come up with....a BIG HUGE THANK YOU. I feel I live in your hearts and you live in mine. Thank you for gracing my life.

So much love!!!!!
leslye/Mukti

December 19, 2022

Hello my beautiful family…. I wanted to let you know I feel this incredible net holding me, this net that is constructed with your love and power and strength…which allows me to feel these tears of joy and to let you know the tears running down my face are tears of gratitude and love, not sadness. I am filled with so much love and to hear you all speak these words…well, I cannot hold my feelings in…I overflow with the love you offer me. You walk into the deep sanctuary of my heart and soul and I feel immersed in your love.
Thank you, thank you, thank you.
Yes, I face fears…and you help me so deeply. I could never have imagined so much.
Thank you,

December 24, 6:50am

Leslye/Mukti breathed her last breath and left her physical body. She was liberated from the pain and suffering she had been experiencing in her body and freed to return to the spirit realm.

Spoken at the cremation ceremony by Steve
(some was adapted from words of Rudolf Steiner)

With deeply moved hearts and weighed down with
grief, we are here by the mortal remains of our
beloved Mukti, Oma for some and Leslye for
some. Mom for others.
She sought with serious striving throughout her life
on earth and now we look up to her soul as it
hastens away, back into spirit realms from which
its came.

We,
Your heart's companions,
Who rejoice in your soul,
Who admire your will,
We gaze
Toward your soul, now released from time.
May you remain
Our eternal companion on the way.

You,
Spirit in the light-filled heights,
May you preserve for us
In endless spirit realms
What united us with you
In the earthly region.

You gave us a gift of love
And faithful spiritual friendship.
May your spirit in the light-filled heights
Make our hearts strong.
So that we may show ourselves
Worthy of the gift
That the gods have given us.

Now we offer our warmth and gratitude and love
as she is leaving the earthly realm and soaring to
spirit lands.

We know we will remain deeply and for all time
united with the being our our dear one, she who
united herself with us while on earth in devoted
love and spiritual fellowship.

You gave us the gift of your being.
I hope we all find that our hearts are strong
So we may become worthy of the gift.

Our love streams toward you
In peace filled devotion,
Seeking to carry you,
To warm your cold,
To cool your heat,
And to light your way
Wanting to support you
In the heights of hope and In the spheres of love.

Epilogue:

Sometime after her passing, as I was collecting these various writings to include in this book, I found something written to me that I think is worthy of sharing with you. Leslye has worked with a letter writing coach to help her write just what she wanted in letters to her grandchildren. I didn't know they had also worked together on a letter to me. I share it here as a closing to this compilation because to me it distills the journey, even though it was a personal message to me. It seems a fitting close to this chronicle and is on the following two pages.

Love given and received never goes away, we carry it in our hearts and it guides us toward the light.

Steve,

*You are teaching me to trust, and just in time.
You know my story. You know I've had a hard time
trusting, believing that anyone could love me. Yet
there you are. Loving me every step of the way. It's
curious that cancer taught me this – taught me that
it doesn't matter if I went to college, or I'm not
witty, or if I'm not Jane Goodall – that none of it
matters because, in fact, I've been loved.
You have been by my side every step of the way.
You've been there for everything.
The spider in the bed, the centipede in the toilet,
my fear of flying, and now this.*

*You sleep by my side in the hospital in
uncomfortable chairs, you come to all my
treatments.
I see everything you've done for me. In your
actions I can see how much you care.
It's not just what you've done, Steve. It's who you
are. I love you even if you didn't do all that you do
for me. What you do is a reflection of who you are
and I see it.
I feel so fortunate, so blessed.
I have a lot of my own wounds around trust, and
it's time to let them go. I feel myself opening to
allow love. It is not without fear - that is probably
why I guarded myself, but it is time, time to allow
myself to love so much, so much that I can be
afraid of losing it, but more afraid of not having had
it, not having held it and treasured it.
I consider this healing that I've been having is a
mixture of things: Kind doctors, exercise, love,
family, and in a way you are a big slice of the
healing pie. There's a different between healing
and cure for me. I've had a big healing in so many
ways.*

You've made a difference. You've made me different. I'm sorry it took me so long to be vulnerable and to open up and feel love and give love, to express gratitude.
But it didn't take forever... Steve, I love you so much. I want to be sure you know this.
Now and forever.

Om shanti, shanti, shanti